DID ADAM AND EVE HAVE BELLY BUTTONS?

*...and 199 other questions
from Catholic teenagers!*

MATTHEW J. PINTO

ASCENSION
PRESS

Published by
Ascension Press
P.O. Box 1840
West Chester, PA 19380
AscensionP@aol.com
1-800-376-0520

Cover design by
Kinsey Advertising, Albuquerque, NM

Published in the United States of America
ISBN# 0-9659228-0-4

To my wife Maryanne.
Thank you for your steadfast love and support.
You are a gift from God.

Merry Christmas 1999
Mike, Dan, Tim
& Jeff

Love,
Uncle John, Aunt Pat,
Kelly, Kristen & Brian
♡ ♡ ♡ ♡ ♡ ♡

Prayer Before Reading

Come Holy Spirit, fill the hearts of Thy faithful
and enkindle in them the fire of Thy love.
Send forth Thy spirit and they shall be created,
And Thou shalt renew the face of the earth.

O God, Who did instruct the hearts of the faithful
by the light of the Holy Spirit,
grant us by the same Spirit to have a right judgement
in all things and ever to rejoice in His consolation.
Through Christ our Lord.
Amen.

Contents

Foreword

There is no doubt about it, young people today are on a quest for truth and happiness. And I believe they're seeing that only in God will they find it (CCC #27). Nearly every day someone calls or writes me requesting a dynamic book for teens that will lead them to God. Parents want a book to give their teens that will help answer life's difficult questions in a format that teens will appreciate. Teens want a book they could give to their friends with inquiring hearts. The book you hold is such a book.

Teens today are faced with more complex questions than generations past while, at the same time, distinguishing truth in popular culture is more difficult as trend setters speak and paint in shades of gray. Perhaps even more dangerous yet is when the message and techniques of Church youth leaders cannot be distinguished from secular humanism or the New Age Movement. The simplicity and clarity of this book, both in style and content, will be refreshing to those who have to continually battle for the truth in their own backyard.

One thing that makes this book so relevant and useful is the fact that the questions asked are real questions submitted by today's teens. Matthew Pinto doesn't shy away from difficult topics and he gives straightforward answers, in harmony with the Church, which include citations from the Bible and the *Catechism of the Catholic Church*. Readers will appreciate both the scope of questions and the succinct answers.

This handy tool will help young Catholics understand and defend their faith and, most importantly, it will better equip them to live a holy life consecrated to Jesus Christ. This book is valuable for personal study and can be used as a reference tool for evangelization as well as an aid for youth leaders in their lesson preparation.

Those who know the author are impressed with his energy and enthusiasm in his work with young people. He knows how they think and the social and spiritual situations they face. As a popular youth speaker, Matt Pinto is a master at applying the truths of the Church to the ever changing moral and social landscape. And now he brings his energy, enthusiasm, and skills to the written page.

So begin the journey. If you are a teenager, read with an open mind and then, if inspired and convinced by the answers, act on them by becoming a soldier for our Lord. If you are a parent or teacher, read the book yourself and then pass it on. The answers contained herein are for all.

— Jeff Cavins
Host, Life on the Rock

Introduction

I started my own advertising business fresh out of college. I wanted success *and I wanted it quickly.* Working 60-70 hours a week for my first three years, the fruits of my labor began to show. I was on my way to wealth and recognition at a young age.

But something unexpected happened — I was growing discontented with the way my life was going. Living only for personal gain, I felt empty and shallow. I was burning out at the ripe old age of 24.

I turned to my Catholic Faith to fill the void. I searched out a young adult group at a nearby parish. It was there that I crashed head on into Catholic truth. Dynamic young Catholics showed me there was more to life than material gain. I learned that I could gain the whole world and lose my soul in the process (Mark 8:36).

I wasted no time in embracing the Faith. Intense about most things, I began an aggressive study of Christianity. That first year, I must have read or studied over 1,000 hours. I replaced my time-management and motivational cassette tapes with theology tapes by Bishop Fulton Sheen and Fr. Ken Roberts. I even stopped dating to "clear my mind" from all distractions. I was on fire.

For the first time in my life I knew who I was. I was a child of God, a Christian, a CATHOLIC! I no longer felt a void in my life. My identity, confidence, and purpose were firmly established. A short time later, I sold my business to work full-time for the Church.

Why tell you all this? Since then I have seen many conversions similar to my own. Through my involvement with youth and young adult ministry, I have seen hundreds of teens and "GenXers" come to the same surety of faith after being introduced to the powerful, life-changing teachings of Jesus Christ and the Catholic Church.

These teens and young adults were taught clear Catholic truth and they responded enthusiastically. The Faith was not "watered down."

Contrary to popular belief, young people don't run from the "tough" teachings (or get bored in CCD class) when Catholic truth is presented clearly and with conviction. Young Catholics are looking for a rock on which they can stand. They're looking for a firm foundation in a changing world. The Church's teaching offers this rock-solid foundation.

Without a firm understanding of Catholic truth, our young Catholics will flounder. They will be unsure about who they are and what they stand for. Our young Catholics will remain quiet at dinner parties when Uncle Louie bad-mouths the Church. They won't speak up when their friends promote pre-marital sex or contemplate abortion, or when non-Catholic missionaries come knocking on the door.

But with apologetics training (the art of defending or giving reasons for one's belief), Catholics, young and old, *will* speak up. They'll be ready to explain, share and charitably defend the Faith (1 Pet. 3:15).

This is a book of Catholic apologetics. It was written to equip young Catholics and give them what has been given to me.

It's composed of serious questions from actual teenagers, including, believe it or not, the question chosen as the title. I try to give serious answers and present Catholic truth in a clear manner. By knowing and living the truth, our young people will be set free from the spirit of the age (John 8:12), and will have a more abundant life (John 10:10).

The book's format makes it an easy read. You can read straight through or hop around to questions that most interest you. Use the book at your youth group, R.C.I.A. or other religious education classes.

Pray before you read. If you are sincerely seeking the truth, God will lead you there. Simply ask and He will respond (Matt. 7:7).

— Matthew J. Pinto

Chapter 1
God

Question #1

"Is there really a God?" Stephen C., 15

A. Yes. God is the ultimate reality. He is actually holding all things in existence. If God stopped doing so, we would cease to exist but He would continue to exist.

We know God exists through revelation (Scripture and Sacred Tradition) and our own intellects (reflecting on the world God made). In the Bible, God reveals: "I Am, Who Am" (Ex. 3:14) and "I am the Alpha and the Omega," (Rev. 1:8) which means He is the beginning and end of all things. Lastly, God has some harsh words for those who deny He exists: "The fool says in his heart that there is no God" (Psalm 14:1).

Question #2

"Other than the Bible, how do we know God exists?" Travis C., 14

A. St. Thomas Aquinas says we can know of God by reason alone. He gives five proofs for the existence of God. I'll give you one of them and then challenge you to read his works to find out the other four.

One proof or argument is from "design." This proof says the universe could not have just come together on its own any more than, say, a computer just "comes together" on its own. The computer is a precise instrument that could not magically come together on its own. It is created and designed by something greater than itself — man. We know God exists by His handiwork. Only an all-powerful God could have orchestrated the creation of the universe, the earth, man and everything else.

Question #3

"Who is God?" Jan Rio P., 14

A. God is our Creator, our Redeemer and our Sanctifier. God is the Blessed Trinity — three distinct Persons Who share the same Divine nature. God is an eternal family. God is love.

Question #4

"What is the nature of God?" Nathan T., 15

God is the Supreme Being. He is self-existing (not caused), eternal, all-powerful, all-knowing and present everywhere. He is pure spirit, which means He does not have the limitations of a body. God is also supremely personal. He is no mere force or power. In fact, He is a communion of Persons — Father, Son and Holy Spirit. This is the Blessed Trinity. All three Persons possess the one divine nature.

Question #5

"What made God so great?" Maria B., 14

A. His mere existence makes Him great. If you're God, you are the greatest of all beings. Being the greatest is a requirement for the "job" of being God. Also, the proof of His greatness is evident all around us in His creation. Do you know one human who has created a real sunset?

Question #6

"What does God look like?" Rachel P., 13

A. God the Father is a pure spirit, which means He has no body. We can't then really describe what He "looks like" because that phrase assumes God the Father has a body like ours that we could "look at." Because it is hard for us to think of a being without a body, God has given us images or descriptions of Himself which help us picture what He is like. For example, we can think of God as a loving Father who cares for and cherishes His children.

The best "picture" of God, however, is Jesus Himself Who said, "Whoever who has seen Me, has seen the Father" (John 14:9). As God the Son, Jesus showed

us what God the Father is like. He also showed us
the Father's perfect love by teaching people, healing the sick, forgiving sins, and, most of all, dying
for our sins on the cross. Jesus promised us that, if
we love God, one day we will "see" Him in the
Beatific Vision, which means that our hearts and
minds will be perfectly united with God in heaven.
In this "vision of God," we will be completely happy
and at peace: We will want nothing.

Question #7

"How did God create Himself?" John D., 14

A. He didn't. He always existed. Creation means to
make something from nothing. To create something
requires that the creator exist before the thing created. When a carpenter makes a table, for example,
he exists before the table he makes. For God to create Himself, He would have to exist before Himself,
which doesn't make any sense.

God could not have been created by someone else,
because then God's creator would be greater than
God. And that doesn't make sense because God is
the supreme or highest Being, and you can't go any
higher than the highest.

Question #8

"What does the Church mean when it re-
fers to God as 'the Father?'" Rocky P., 15

A. The Church means that, although God is a pure spirit and not literally male, we speak of God in male terms because God's relation to us is like that of a Father. This doesn't mean men are better than women, only that some aspects of "maleness" better express some aspects of God's relationship to us than "femaleness." Both men and women are, however, made in God's image.

Why does the Church call God "Father?" One reason is Jesus. Our relation to God is a sharing in *Jesus'* relation to God. He knew and revealed God *as Father*. Therefore, that's how we should know and relate to God. Jesus couldn't know God as Mother for a simple reason: He already had a Mother, the Blessed Virgin Mary. As Jesus' brothers and sisters, we too have Mary as a spiritual Mother. And God is our spiritual Father, a fatherhood more real than even our biological relationship with our own earthly fathers.

Another reason we call God "Father" has to do with His relation to us as His creatures. If we think of the whole creation as our mother — as, say, "Mother Earth" or "Mother Nature" — then God's relation to us is like that of a father.

Think of it this way: God is related to creation like a husband to his wife or bridegroom to his bride. We, as individuals, are sort of God's offspring through the rest of creation, the way children are offspring of their father by their mother. God brings us into existence "outside" of Himself but "inside" (or as a part) of the rest of creation, His spouse, so to speak. This is like how a father procreates new life outside himself, within his wife. And creation sustains us and provides a place for us to live. This is like how a mother procreates new life inside herself from her husband, like how she nurtures and cares for children within her womb.

The *Catechism of the Catholic Church* states that God's Fatherhood includes the perfections of human fatherhood and motherhood. And the Bible also sometimes describes God's love in maternal ways (Isaiah 49:15; 66:13). So we shouldn't be afraid of all maternal *imagery* as a way of understanding God's love for us, provided it is properly understood. However, neither the Bible nor the *Catechism* ever calls God "mother." And even when maternal images are used in the Bible, God remains "He" not "She" (CCC #239).

Naturally, there is much more, but this overview should give you at least a basic understanding of this important issue.

Question #9

Q. "How do I know that God loves me?" Kyle T., 14

A. Because He made you in His image and likeness,

which He did not have to do. Quite simply, God made you because He knew you would like it. God needs no companions. He does not need our praise. His creation of us was a gift.

He also made you because He wants you to experience the bliss and unspeakable joy that will come from spending eternity with Him.

We also know God loves us because Scripture says, "God so loved the world that He sent His only Son so that everyone who believes in Him might not perish but might have eternal life" (John 3:16). If He did not give His Son as the ultimate sacrifice for sin, we all would have perished in hell because of sin. Sending His Son was an act of love.

Question #10

"Will God always love you no matter what you do?" Kindra M., 16

A. Yes, but this does not mean you will get to heaven *no matter what you do.* A parent who loves a teenager too much to let him live a destructive life may kick the teenager out of the house. If the teen doesn't seek forgiveness, he may never be allowed back. This is not a perfect analogy (because God doesn't "kick us out" of heaven; we choose to be separated from Him), but it helps demonstrate the point how God does not force salvation on us. He gives us free will to either accept or reject His love. However, He does continually send us grace that works on our hearts and consciences because it is His will that all be saved (1 Tim. 2:4).

If we do not want to be saved and prove this by disobedience, we will not be saved. This does not mean that God doesn't love us. He loves us more than we can know. However, salvation is conditional based on our response to His love. Why? Because "salvation" ultimately means being with God. And God will not force anyone to be with Him who doesn't want to be with Him.

Question #11
"How can God change my life?" Ed R., 17

A. God made you. He knows everything you ever did *or will do*. Scripture says He even knows the number of hairs on your head (Luke 12:7). By humbling ourselves and asking for His guidance, He will lead us to peace and happiness in this life and eternal joy in the next. Not allowing God to work in your life is like swimming upstream — you simply will not get anywhere that *really* counts. All achievements will be in vain. However, with God every action has purpose and meaning.

Question #12
"If God cares for people, how come He lets people kill each other?" Lauren S., 15

A. For the same reason He lets people love each other. He loved us so much that He gave us the tremendous gift of free will.

God wants human beings to choose Him freely. He doesn't want to force Himself on us. God gave us wills so we would be able to experience some of the joy He knows as God. This joy comes from the divine love, and this type of love requires freedom. (Freedom involves the ability to freely give one's self to another.) You cannot force such love; not even God can force us to love Him in this sense.

Man cannot be free to love God without having, at the same time, the freedom to reject Him. With this freedom comes the possibility of evil, which God hates but does allow. It is this free will that enables some men to embrace evil. This can lead to sin, including murder. Rest assured, however, that neither iniquities nor injustices will go unpunished in the eternal courtroom.

Question #13

"Why does God make us suffer from abuse and diseases like cancer?" Caity N., 14

A. God doesn't make us suffer from abuse and disease, although He sometimes *permits* them.

To understand evil, we need to understand God. God has one ultimate "will," but this "will" is expressed in two ways: His *positive* will and His *passive* will. His positive will is what brings about all the good we see. His passive will *allows* evil to happen, but only because God intends to bring about a greater good from it. Evil happens because of man's free choices. God simply allows some of man's choices to bring about their natural consequences. Even so, God can bring greater good from this.

Let's say a man has lived a very selfish life that includes heavy drinking and abuse of his wife. God may allow this man to lose his health because He knows that if the man stays healthy, he will continue to seriously sin. But, if the man is incapacitated, he may come to see the true beauty of his wife, and then may reconcile himself to God and his spouse. Much good can come from suffering if we embrace it when it comes our way.

One final point. God understands our suffering through the suffering of Christ on the cross. We can link our sufferings with the sufferings of Jesus on the cross and, thus, offer them up as gifts to the Father.

Chapter 2
Creation and Man

Question #14
"What is the meaning of life?" Zed R., 13

A. The meaning of life is to know, love and serve God. This is where we will find our fulfillment here on earth and in heaven. Love is the underlying theme throughout the Bible. In fact, there are over 600 verses in Scripture which speak of love.

To begin, the creation of human beings was an act of unselfish love by God. (He didn't need us because He was perfect. But He created us because He knew we would like it.) This was an act of love. We are called to this type of unselfish love.

Love is most fully expressed when we give of ourselves with no interest in gaining something from it. Love is wanting what is best for another *simply because it is best for that person.* Love is the greatest of the virtues (1 Cor. 13:13). Love is the opposite of selfishness. God exhibited the ultimate act of love when He gave His only Son as the definitive sacrifice to save the world from its sins (John 3:16). The Son, Jesus Christ, gave His own life for us when He died on the cross. Love truly makes the world a better place. Without love, we have emptiness.

The meaning of life is love: accepting love from God, giving love back to God through obedience to Him and to love others as we love God and ourselves.

Question #15

"Did God begin or start the whole world? If not, how did the world begin?" Rachel P., 13

A. Yes, God created the whole world. A carpenter makes a chair from wood. A poet makes a poem from words that already exist. Making something implies that the original materials are there first. But God did not merely *make* us. He *created* us from nothing. Although we speak of people *creating*, only God creates in the strictest sense, for only God can bring something from nothing.

God brought the universe into existence from nothing. He creates each and every human soul from nothing at conception.

Why did God create the universe from nothing rather than something? What else would He have created it from? Not from Himself, for there are no parts in

God which He could "break off" to fashion us from. And if He used something else, where would *that* have come from? Being all-powerful, God can do what no one else can: create something from nothing. Scripture says: "He spoke and they were made. He commanded and they were created" (Psalm 148:5).

Question #16

Doesn't the Big Bang theory explain the way the world was created apart from a Creator? Tracy P., 18

A. No, because even if the Big Bang theory is true, it doesn't explain where the matter came from that caused the Big Bang. And even if you hold, as some scientists do, that before the Big Bang that started our universe, there were an infinite number of Big Bangs and Big Collapses or "earlier" universes, exploding and collapsing, you still have a problem. Where did the stuff these Big Bangs and Big Collapses were made of come from? Also, why is the universe the kind of place where there are such occurrences, when it doesn't have to be? Where did the *whole thing* come from, anyway?

Since the universe doesn't explain its own existence, the explanation for it must be somewhere else. And that somewhere else can only be something — actually Someone — who is self-existing, God.

Question #17

"If the sun and the moon mark the days and they were created on the fourth day, how could the other days have come about?"
Nicholas D., 14

A. Your question shows one of the problems with accepting the Genesis story as a complete, literal history of creation. Of course, some of the book of Genesis *is* historical — the existence of Abraham, for example. But, Catholicism allows us to interpret other parts of it figuratively, so long as our interpretations do not contradict other Catholic doctrines.

For example, we aren't forced into the restrictive interpretations of the creation presented by some Protestant Fundamentalists. We don't have to assume all narratives in the opening chapters of Genesis are *strictly* historical or historical in every detail, in order to believe there was a Creation and Fall of Man, for example. When we think of the writer of Genesis (Chapter 1) as expressing the creation of the world in poetic fashion, the problem you mention vanishes.

According to Genesis 1, God created and distinguished light and darkness on the "first day." This "day," however, isn't so much a 24-hour period as a poetic way of showing how God created things in stages, in an orderly fashion, fitting each thing in its proper place. After God created "light," for instance,

He then created realms or places for things — the sky, separating it from the waters covering the earth, the oceans from dry land. Finally, He populated these places with things — first, plants on land, then sun, moon and stars in the sky, and then sea creatures and birds. On the final "day" of creation, God created the land animals, and, after this, man.

As the Genesis writer describes it, God went from the most basic creatures to the highest, most complex — man, made in God's image — creating a place for each beforehand. This shows in a poetic form, rather than in a strictly scientific description, that God created things in an orderly fashion because He is a God of order, not chaos.

So, the historical truth of the Genesis creation story is one thing — God *did* create the world and man. How that truth is recounted, poetically, is another.

Question #18

"Did Adam and Eve have belly buttons?" Gilbert A., 18

A. Your fellow teens may think this is a joke question. It's not. It actually is a very clever question. You are really asking, "If Adam and Eve were created directly by God, they should *not* have belly buttons. But if they evolved from apes, wouldn't they have belly buttons?"

Quite frankly, we just don't know if Adam and Eve had belly buttons. The Church does not speak of whether they did or did not have them because it does not speak officially on *how* creation took place. The Church is mainly concerned with *why* creation took place and *what* the implications are of our creation.

So, although this may be a clever title for a book, we just don't know the answer for sure. You'll have to wait until you get to heaven to find out. (Note: This is one of the few "We don't know." answers in this book.)

Of course, God could have created Adam and Eve with belly buttons, just as He created them mature rather than as children. Instead of whether or not they had belly buttons, perhaps we should ponder an even more profound question: "If they did have belly buttons, would they have been 'innies' or 'outies'"?

Question #19

"Can a Catholic believe in evolution?"
Rebecca G., 17

A. Looking at evolution as the process of *how* God created the world does not pose a problem for the Catholic. However, because some aspects of "evolution" can impact the faith of the believer, the Church does offer guidelines for what must be believed and what is left up to the individual's judgement.

Before considering those guidelines, let's be clear about the difference between "evolution" and "evolutionism." Evolution is a scientific *theory* which says that more complex forms of life developed from less complex forms, over extreme periods of time. As a scientific theory, it is to be accepted or rejected based on the evidence. Evolutionism, on the other hand, is the belief that everything that exists can be explained in exclusively materialist terms, apart from a Creator. According to evolutionism, everything that exists developed from "blind chance" with no knowing or planning of its purpose or end.

Evolutionism is not only unscientific, it is unreasonable because it holds that a complex organism like the human brain developed by "blind chance." Because evolutionism denies the creative action of God, it is dangerous for us to hold to this view. It implies that humans are mere animals.

Here are some guidelines on what the Catholic should believe regarding creation and evolution.

The first three chapters of Genesis contain elements of historical truth, even though the inspired author may have used a poetic literary form to communicate these truths. When I say "historical truth," I mean something that really happened. The first sin (original sin) really happened at a certain time and place in history. Perhaps it was six thousand years ago; perhaps six hundred thousand years ago. For all we know, the first sin may well have had something to do with eating a certain fruit which God had commanded man not to eat. But it needn't have. That may simply be a poetic way the Genesis writer chose to communicate the historical truth about man's fall from paradise. What we must affirm is that there really was a first sin.

We must also affirm the following:

1) All things were created by a loving God.

2) Man is made in the image of God, which means, among other things, that he is a spiritual being, with the powers of knowing and freely choosing.

3) Even if man's body evolved, God still created man because God created the process of evolution and His providence guided it to give rise to the human race.

4) Whatever the origin of man's bodily form, his soul is a special creation of God, not the result of an evolutionary process. This is because spirit, unlike matter, is incapable of evolving, since it has no parts to evolve from one thing to another.

5) We all descended from one original set of parents.

6) Our original parents were created in a state of happiness.

7) Their obedience was tested and they transgressed the divine law at the prompting of the devil.

8) They lost the supernatural gifts given to the human race by God.

9) They passed on original sin to all mankind.

10) They were promised a redeemer.

So long as these basic elements of Catholic teaching on creation are held, Catholics may adopt the theory of evolution. Nevertheless, a Catholic is not obliged to do so, if he or she thinks the evidence is against it. Evolution is a scientific theory, not a theological dogma. It stands or falls on the evidence.

Question #20

"It seems to me that you have to believe that either evolution or creation is true. How can you believe both at the same time as I hear some people say?" Alice B., 15

A. By holding that God used evolution as His way of forming human beings. In that sense, you could say the *only* way a Catholic can believe in evolution is *also* to believe in creation (although the opposite is not true; you can believe in creation without affirming evolution).

When some people, usually Fundamentalist Protestants and atheists, oppose evolution and creation to each other, they usually mean evolution by blind chance vs. creation in the sense of God literally fashioning man from "the dust of the earth" and "breathing" into man the "breath of life." Obviously, creation and evolution in those senses can't both be true. But if evolution is understood as a process designed by God, and creation simply God's act of bringing human beings into existence however it happened, then there needn't be a conflict. It needn't be *either* evolution *or* creation; it can be *both* evolution *and* creation.

People think there is a conflict between science and faith because they think the only alternatives are the strict Fundamentalist view and the atheistic scientific view. Fundamentalists insist the creation story in Genesis must be interpreted as strict history in every detail. For them, it isn't enough to say the Creation and Fall of Man really happened; they insist it must have happened *exactly* as the Genesis writer narrated it, without his intending to put anything poetically or allegorically. Atheistic scientists, on the other hand, say the creation of the human race (and the universe as a whole) was due to blind chance, without any divine intervention, whether by evolution or by any other means. This is a false set of choices.

A Catholic may completely embrace the creation narrative as a historical depiction in every detail, but he is not required by the Church to do so. He may also embrace the evolutionary theory as a scientific explanation, as long as he doesn't deny fundamental Christian truths mentioned in the previous question.

Question #21

"If we were created by God, why do scientists have such strong evidence that we evolved from apes?" Jennie F., 17

A. There is disagreement about just how strong such evidence is. Because evolution has been taught as fact for the past several decades in our schools, most people accept it as true. They don't know about the problems with the theory or evidence that can be interpreted in other ways.

Evolutionary science is not the stable discipline we are led to believe. It involves a lot of self-correction and revision. For example, theories about the variations of early man used to include dividing early man into different types, including Peking man, Java man and Neanderthal man. Today, they are all considered one — *Homo Erectus*. There are no divisions in type. Scientists now see that different fossils (which are few) are essentially the same.

Theories that early man was ferocious are now being refuted because of evidence which shows that early man was quite advanced in the development and use of tools, he performed amputations and even buried the deceased with flowers. These are not acts of a beast.

In 1911, French anatomist Marcellin Boule's Neanderthal skeleton led him to conclude that early man was hunched over with his face thrust forward, similar to the gorilla. Forty-five years later, a team of anatomists re-examined Boule's skeleton and concluded the hunched over stance was not due to genetics, but to severe arthritis.

Because evolutionary scientists cannot test their theories in a controlled laboratory as chemists can, their theories are developed from "reasonable interpretations" and, even, imagination. Fossil evidence needs to be interpreted because it does not speak for itself.

Based on developments from the 1970s to the present, the case for evolution, especially Darwin's theory of natural selection, is being called into serious question by respected scientists. The theory may still be true, but opposing opinions, which were blocked out of academic life because of prejudice and "anti-religious" sentiment, are now being heard. If you're interested in learning more, I recommend reading *Darwin on Trial* by Philip Johnson or Michael Behe's *Darwin's Black Box.* Both are listed in the "Resources" section at the end of this book.

Chapter 3
Religion and the Bible

Question #22

"How did we get the Bible?" Ryan C., 16

A. There are two answers to your question — one from history, the other from theology. We don't have space here to go into detail about the history of the Bible. Suffice it to say that the Bible as we know it today was composed over a period of almost a thousand years. The Old Testament books were written mainly in Hebrew; the New Testament in Greek. They were copied by hand and preserved with remarkable accuracy, as archeological findings such as the Dead Sea Scrolls confirm.

The theological answer to your question is easier to state: God inspired the biblical writers to write the Bible we have today. That means without revoking their freedom, God so moved them that they wrote what He wanted them to write. In that sense, God is the primary Author of the Bible with the human authors serving as His instruments. This is the doctrine of biblical inspiration. It means the Bible is the Word of God without ceasing also to be the words of men.

You may want to look at some short books that trace the Bible's history. The first is *Where We Got the Bible* (Catholic Answers). The second is a short booklet, *How the Bible Has Come to Us* (Scepter Press). Lastly, *The Catholic Church and the Bible* (Ignatius Press) is an excellent resource as well. Addresses for the publishers of these works are in the "Resources" section of this book.

Question #23

"How do we know the Bible is the written Word of God?" Thang P., 19

A. We know the Bible is inspired because the Catholic Church has constantly taught that it is, and we have Jesus' promise that He won't allow the Church to err on such a basic issue (Matt. 16:18-19). But, someone might ask, how do we know, apart from the Bible, that Jesus promised He would preserve the Church from erring on such things? And if we have to rely on the Bible to know that, isn't this circular reasoning: using the Bible to support the Church and the Church to justify the Bible?

No, it isn't a circular argument to rely on the Bible here, but a "spiral" one. Let me explain: We start with the Bible as a purely historical record (the general reliability of which we can defend on historical grounds without appealing to revelation) to show who Jesus is — the Son of God. (The argument for Christ's divinity we have to assume for the moment.) Then we show that He told His followers He would guide them and that He even chose apostles to do so. In other words, He established a teaching authority in the Church and endowed it with His special guidance. Again, at this point, we're using the Bible as a simple historical record of what happened, not as the inspired Word of God.

Next, we show that the Church Christ promised to guide has declared certain writings to be inspired. The list of inspired books which the Church put together is called the Canon of Scripture, ("canon" with one "n," which means a standard of measure, not something you shoot).

Because Christ is the Son of God, when He promises something, He has the power to make sure it happens. He promised to guide His followers and to do it through the apostles. The apostles in turn passed along a share in their authority to the bishops, who eventually officially declared the biblical books to be inspired. Their declaration didn't, of course, make the Bible inspired; God did that when He moved men to write the various books. What the Church did was to settle once and for all which books are divinely inspired. And she did it with the authority of Christ, Who promised to be with her.

This argument is based on faith that Christ is Who He claimed and that He will do as he promised. Believing these things isn't blind faith — faith *opposed* to reason or *without* reason. True, we can't fully "see" from reason alone that Christ is the Son of God, but this doesn't make faith in such things unreasonable. Faith is *supra*-rational (above reason), not irrational (against reason).

There's another approach to the Bible's inspiration we can take. We can show how certain things are best explained on the premise the Bible is the inspired, written Word of God. The fulfillment of biblical prophecy, for example. Doesn't that suggest the Scripture has a more than human origin? Of course, this approach doesn't *absolutely* prove the inspiration of the Bible, but it does strongly support the idea.

Question #24

"What is the difference between the Old and New Testaments?" Alyssa W., 14

A. The Old Testament is the collection of books that record the story of the creation of man; the fall of man through sin; the giving of the Law (including the Ten Commandments); the promise of God given to us through the prophets of a messiah (Jesus); the life and trials of the chosen people — the Jews, as they struggled to be faithful while waiting for the messiah; and the events leading up to the birth of Jesus.

The Old Testament contains 46 books which are traditionally divided into four categories: the Pentateuch, the historical books, the wisdom books and the prophetic books. A list of the books in each of these categories can usually be found in the instructional pages of your Bible.

The New Testament begins with the birth of Jesus, but it tells us little about the life of Christ before He began His public ministry around age 30.

The New Testament can also be divided into four kinds of writing: gospels (summaries of Jesus' life and teaching), the letters (called epistles) of various apostles and apostolic men (Paul, Peter, James, John, Jude and the author of Hebrews) to early Catholic communities, the Acts of the Apostles (a history of the early Christians) and the Apocalypse (Revelation). There are 27 books in the New Testament.

In short, the Old Testament is the story of the Jewish people and the New Testament is the story of the Catholic people who were both Jews and Gentiles (non-Jews) who accepted and followed Christ.

Question #25

"Are the stories in the Bible true?" Stephen C., 15

A. Yes, all stories in the Bible are true, but not all are intended to give us *historical* truth. The parables of

Jesus contain life-changing truths that can lead us to a deeper understanding of God and His message of repentance, love and truth. But that doesn't mean things described in the parables necessarily really happened. We don't have to think there really was a prodigal son, for example. (Although it may very well have happened as it is written.)

On the other hand, when the biblical author intended to say that something really did happen, then it did. The gospel writers intended to say that Jesus Christ really lived, suffered, died and literally rose from the dead. That isn't a parable, and they didn't intend it to be viewed as one.

Whether a given story is history, then, depends on the intent of the author in telling it. How do we know what the writer intended? That requires properly interpreting the Bible, which is mainly the job of bishops and scholars who help them.

Question #26

"What does the Bible have to offer the world today?" Nathan T., 15

A. The Bible offers the living Word of God to all people in all ages. That living Word is Christ Himself. Christ fully reveals us to ourselves. He shows us why we are here and where we are headed. The Bible brings Christ to us. Through Jesus we can know the meaning and purpose of life.

The truth of Christ presented in the Bible can remedy the world's ills and bring us to everlasting happiness with God and peace with ourselves.

Question #27

"Why is religion so important in our lives?" Jeff H., 14

A. It depends on what you mean by "religion." Not all religions are true or equally true, so religion *as such* is neither good nor bad. If by "religion" you mean the truths about God and man's relation to Him, that *is* important because it's true. It's the way things are. True religion is important because it helps us to know the Ultimate Reality, God.

True religion is also important because it helps us fulfill our purpose, both as individuals and as a society. God made us for a purpose and unless we consult what He has revealed about that purpose and live accordingly, we shall be failed creatures, as useless as a screen door on a submarine or a bathing suit in a snow storm.

Because true religion reveals why we're here, it shows us the meaning of life. It can keep us from despair and prepare us for the fulfillment of our existence in the next life. It also provides guidelines for human society. Imagine what things would be like without the moral laws and principles true religion provides. Everyone would do what he or she selfishly liked without any regard for others. This would lead to complete self-indulgence, which leads to all types of vice and sin. True religious belief teaches us to get out of ourselves and turn to God and others.

Question #28

"Why are religion and church so boring?" Colin M., 16

A. They're not. If God made all things and, subsequently, knows the meaning of all things, how could the study of God possibly be boring? *We* sometimes make them boring, but they are not boring when properly taught and seriously studied.

Sometimes we're addicted to superficial kinds of excitement — that's one drawback of so much television and its never-ending stimulation. When it comes to really important things like God, why we exist and where we're headed, we yawn and flip the TV channel to watch some mindless sitcom that has phony track laughter in the background.

But sooner or later, the realities of life catch up with us and we're forced to face the RBQs — Really Big Questions. Then we see that religion and church are anything but boring because they help us answer these questions.

Chapter 4
Jesus Christ

Question #29

"Is Jesus God or is He God's son?" Melissa D., 15

A. He is both. To say Jesus is God means He is a divine person, the second person of the Trinity and He possesses the divine nature — He acts as God acts. To say He is the Son of God means He is the Son of the Father, the first person of the Trinity, and He possesses the divine nature from the Father.

Perhaps this analogy will help. As a human being, you are the child of human parents, not mere animal parents. You possess a human nature from them. Well, Jesus is the eternal Son of the Father. He existed with the Father as the divine Son before being born in Bethlehem 2,000 years ago. In fact, He existed from all eternity with the Father, eternally proceeding from Him as light streams forth from the sun. And as you share a common human nature with your parents, so the Son shares the divine nature with God the Father (and the Holy Spirit). In that sense, we can speak of Jesus as being the Son of God because He is God the Son, second person of the Trinity.

There is, however, another sense in which Jesus is the Son of God. Jesus Christ possesses two natures, a human nature and a divine nature. Jesus is also the Son of God in the sense that God alone is the Father of His human nature. The doctrine of the Virginal Conception and Birth holds that Jesus had no earthly father.

Another thing to keep in mind is that Jesus is not 50 percent human and 50 percent divine. He is 100 percent human and 100 percent divine. This joining of the two natures is called the Hypostatic Union.

Question #30

"How do we know Jesus even existed?" Dave G., 14

A. How do we know George Washington or Abraham Lincoln ever existed? We were not there. We rely on history and records from that period. So too with Christ. The primary record of His existence is the Bible. Although we Christians usually think of the Bible as the Word of God, we should remember much of it is a historical record as well. The New Testament documents in particular give us vital historical information about Jesus, even though they aren't intended to be extensive biographies in the modern sense.

The New Testament picture of Jesus is supported by non-Christian historical sources, although there aren't many of these that survived from the time of the early Church. The probable reason for such scant non-Christian historical evidence is that the Romans, who were the main historians of the time, would not have been concerned with a small outpost of their empire like Palestine. The Jewish historian Josephus does record the existence of Jesus and the fact He was executed under Pontius Pilate. This corroborates the New Testament account.

Question #31

"Why was Jesus killed on the cross?" Steven O., 13

A. Because many of the Jewish priests and elders at that time, as well as pagan Roman leaders, were greatly disturbed and threatened by His message. The Jewish leaders saw Him as a threat to the Jewish Law. The Roman leaders were concerned that He would cause a political uprising.

Question #32

"Why does Jesus love us so much?" Clare M., 16

A. Because He is God. God loves us perfectly. Our finite minds can't grasp the infinite. This is why we will never fully understand why God loves us so much. The evidence of His love for us is that He died for our sins. Scripture says: "No one has greater love than this, to lay down one's life for one's friends" (John 15:13). Jesus' death for us on the cross was the supreme act of love.

One other reason why we know Jesus loves us is because He made us. This is an act of love.

Question #33

"Is there any record of how Jesus was in His younger years, ages 10-12, etc.?" Charity W., 17

A. The only thing we know of Jesus' younger years was when, at age 12, He was found by His parents in the temple discussing matters with the priests and elders. Upon finding Jesus, His parents asked, "Son, why have You done this to us? Your father and I have been looking for You with great anxiety." To which Jesus responded, "Why were you looking for Me? Did you not know that I must be in My Father's house" (Luke 2:49)? The story goes on to say how He left with His parents and was obedient to them. The fact that the God-man would be obedient to His parents offers us a valuable lesson.

There are claims of private revelations (vs. public revelation which is revealed in Scripture and the Tradition of the Church) about Jesus' early years, but

Catholics aren't obliged to accept them. Also, they may include serious errors about Christ so we should be cautious.

Question #34

"Assuming Jesus was God, is He responsible for all things? For example, did Jesus build my hot rod?" Matthew S., 16

A. No, a mechanic built it. But all creation comes from God, and Jesus is God, so all creation *ultimately* comes from Jesus.

God made the matter out of which your car was made. He made the man who made the car. He gave him intellect and freedom to acquire the skill to make your car. God permitted the circumstances in which the man used his skills to make your car. Finally, God sustains your hot rod in existence, moment by moment. Let's not claim more for your car than that.

Chapter 5

Catholicism and "The Church"

Question #35

"Why be a Catholic?" Justin M., 15

A. Being a Catholic is how you fulfill the purpose of your existence: to know God and to be united with Him. The means that God has given us to enter that relationship with Him is faith in and obedience to His Son Jesus. This obedience includes following Jesus' commands, including receiving Baptism.

The way we know and love Jesus is through His Church, which He established to teach, sanctify and shepherd people in His name. That means He wants you to belong to the Catholic Church. Why else would He go to the trouble of establishing it?

Through the teaching of the Church, Christ gives us His truth without error (infallibly). Through the Sacraments and prayer of the Church, Christ gives us His grace and sanctifies us. Through the pastoral authority of the Church, Christ governs and shepherds us as His people.

Question #36

"Can you give a brief history of our faith?" Erin O., 15

A. Jesus was the Messiah for Whom the Jews were waiting. Approximately 2,000 years ago, He was born of a virgin. Around age 33, He was unjustly put to death. Three days later, Jesus rose from the dead. Before He ascended into heaven, He established the Catholic Church on Peter, the first pope, whom Jesus called the "rock" (Matt. 16:18).

The Faith started out small, but grew as people saw the wonderful changes in lifestyle and the heroic martyrdoms of the first Catholics. Around the year 313, Constantine decreed that Christianity could be legally practiced. Around the year 390, the Church established the final version of the Bible. Over the first 1,000 years of the Church's history there were many heresies that sprouted up. These forced the Church to define and clarify its doctrines.

In the year 1054, a major split occurred between the Eastern and Western Catholic Churches. The Eastern Church is still separated from us. They are referred to as the Eastern Orthodox Church.

One of the most devastating events in Christian history came at the hands of a monk named Martin Luther. In his attempt to correct some of the abuses in the Church (and some would say to address his psychological problem of scrupulosity), he broke away from the Church and established a new system of theology. He promoted a new doctrine called *Sola Scriptura*, which basically said that we don't need a Church to guide us to Christian truth. One simply needed to interpret the Bible on his own to find out what is and is not true. This new doctrine led to chaos. Today, there are over 20,000 Protestant Churches that have been founded because of this man-made tradition of "private interpretation."

From the 1500s until the present, the Church has continued to grow. It nourished many of the institutions and disciplines we have today, including art, music, the law system, farming techniques, architecture, formalized schooling, and more. In fact, most historians would admit that the Catholic Church is clearly the most influential organization in the history of the world.

Naturally, there is much more. The life of the Church is more intriguing than any soap opera or novel you could read. It has saints and sinners. It has been heroic and cowardly. But, despite any human failings, the Church is still the bride of Christ. And, if anything is standing at the end of time, it will be the Church because it alone has been given the gifts of infallibility, indefectibility and indestructibility.

For a good short book on the Church's history, I

recommend *A Short History of the Catholic Church* by Jose Orlandis, which I've listed in the "Resouces" section.

Question #37

"How do you prove that Catholicism is the 'correct' religion to believe in?" Jennie F., 17

A. First you have to conclude that Jesus was God and the Messiah the world was waiting for. You then need to find out which church is the one true Church He established. To do this, you should look for the church that has *all* the aspects of the Church identified in Scripture.

Let's first address the question of whether Jesus was God. When considering this question, we can only conclude one of three things: 1) He was a liar, 2) He was a lunatic, or 3) He was Lord. Let me try to succinctly point out He had to be God or Lord.

To begin, Jesus said He was God in several places in Scripture (John 1:1, 5:18; Phil 2:6; Col. 1:15-19) and performed dozens of recorded miracles to substantiate His claim, including walking on water (Matt. 14:25), feeding the 5,000 with just a few loaves of bread and fishes (Mk. 6:34-44), and raising people from the dead (Matt 9:18-26, John 11:1-44). In addition, 10 of the 12 apostles died as martyrs for this belief. (Judas betrayed Jesus and hanged himself, and the apostle John died a natural death.) The 10 apostles who chose to be killed would not have done this had they not believed He was the Messiah or seen Him prove His divinity by His miracles.

Jesus cannot be a liar because He chose to die a brutal death and turned down several requests for world power. A liar (or opportunist) would do neither. He cannot be a madman or "crazy" because His teachings were rational and His thinking was calculated and very clear.

Assuming then that He was God, we need to look for what He came to do. Scripture reveals He came to die for our sins (1 Tim. 2:5-6, Heb. 2:17) and establish a Church that would teach in His name when He went to heaven (Matt. 18:17 and 16:18, 1 Tim. 3:15).

To find the true Church, we need also to look at Scripture and history. Regarding Scripture, all Catholic doctrines are either explicitly or implicitly supported by Scripture. Nothing the Church teaches, when properly understood, goes against Scripture or reason. Furthermore, only the Catholic Church fits completely the pattern of the Church in the New Testament. Only the Catholic Church is visibly one in Faith, in Sacraments and in Church government with the successor of St. Peter, the pope.

A strong case for Catholicism is also made by studying history. If you look at the extra-biblical writings of the early Christians, you will see they taught Catholic doctrines. In fact, the Roman Catholic Church was often referred to by name. The first recorded usage of the word "catholic" is found as early as 107 A.D. A disciple of the apostle John, Ignatius of Antioch, said: "Wherever the bishop appears, let the people be there, just as wherever Jesus Christ is, there is the catholic church." The Catholic Church can trace its authority as the one true church through its unbroken line of over 260 popes from John Paul II back to St. Peter. All other Christian churches are ultimately offshoots of the Catholic Church and were founded by mere men or women, not by Jesus, who was God in the flesh.

Question #38

"Is the Catholic religion the only correct religion?" Beth R., 14

A. All religions contain some truth. Some religions contain more truth than others. For example, Protestant Christianity is much closer to the truth than Mormonism because Protestants believe there is one God, whereas Mormonism incorrectly teaches there are many gods. Eastern Orthodoxy contains more truth than Protestantism, because in addition to the basic Christian beliefs such as the divinity of Jesus and the Virgin Birth, it affirms Jesus' Real Presence in the Eucharist, honors the saints who have died before us and affirms many other Catholic beliefs.

The Catholic Church says that although other faiths contain truth, the *fullness* of what God has revealed to the world *subsists* in (is found in) the Catholic Church. Other religions or faiths are correct to the extent they hold the revealed truths given to the apostles and passed on to the present-day bishops in the Catholic Church.

This does not mean in order to be saved one has to be a "card-carrying member" of the Catholic Church. God can save whomever He desires and has surely done so outside the visible structure of the Catholic Church. However, the *surest* means to salvation is found in the Catholic Church. Its doctrines are the ones infallibly given by Jesus.

Question #39

"Why is the Catholic Church so close-minded?" Ellie M., 17

A. As Catholic apologist G.K. Chesterton said, the purpose of an open mind, like that of an open mouth, is to close it on something solid. For the mind, that "something solid" is truth. When we don't know the truth but seek it, we're free to be (in fact, we should be) open minded. But once we've come to a firm conviction of the truth of something, to remain "open minded" about it is foolishness. Most people aren't "open-minded" about whether murder is good or theft bad. They've made up their minds and rightly so.

When it comes to religious issues, the Catholic Church has "made up its mind." There are good reasons for what the Church teaches, so it isn't a matter of "close-mindedness" in the wrong sense. It's a question of a reasoned conviction.

Another important point to remember: The Catholic Faith comes from God. Neither the pope and the other bishops, nor the priests and deacons, nor the laity are free to change Catholicism to appear "open minded." Their job is simply to tell people the truth in a loving manner. They don't make up or determine the truth for themselves.

Question #40

"How does one become a Catholic?" Jennifer F., 14

A. I assume you mean teenagers or adults, not babies. First a person studies the Faith. Then if he or she chooses to embrace it, he or she will make a formal profession of faith, accepting what the Church teaches as true. Next, the person will be baptized (if he or she hasn't been already). Usually, the new convert will also receive the other Sacraments of initiation, Confirmation and the Holy Eucharist, at this time. Those already validly baptized make a profession of Faith and then receive Confirmation, Confession and the Holy Eucharist.

If you are interested in becoming a Catholic you

should contact the local parish to find out what steps need to be taken. I also recommend reading good books like Father John Hardon's *The Faith*, which is an instruction book based on the new *Catechism*, to help supplement the education you'll receive at the parish. I've listed this book in the "Resources" section.

Chapter 6
Catholicism and Other Faiths

Question #41

"If you get confirmed, could you join another faith, such as Baha'i, later on?" Alice B., 15

A. Confirmation is a statement that you freely choose to be a "soldier for Christ" and the Catholic Church. A real soldier wouldn't fight for both sides. You can't simultaneously profess one faith and then another without violating the laws of logic. Different faiths teach different things or they would be together. Basic logic says if one group says that "X" is true and another says that "X" is false, they both can't be right.

Regarding Baha'i specifically, it was founded by Mirza Husayn 'Ali Huri, who took another name which means "Glory of God." One of the central tenets of this new religion is the "common foundation of all religion." This sounds nice but is an impossibility because of the fundamental differences between religions. Who determines what "common foundations" means? Is that person or group of people infallible? If not, how can we trust their teachings?

There have been thousands of new faiths that have popped up over the past 400 years, especially in the last 100 years. In time, Baha'i, like most of the others, will fall by the wayside. Only the Catholic Church is founded by God Himself (Matt. 16:18) and its teachings will be guided and protected until the end of time (Matt. 28:19-20).

Question #42

"If you leave the Catholic faith for another faith, can you come back to the Church if you don't like the other religion?" Travis G., 15

A. Yes, and you can bet the angels in heaven will be rejoicing when you do. Remember the story of the prodigal son? He came back to his father after living a wild life and spending his inheritance. When his father saw him in the distance, he ran to meet his son, threw his arms around him and gave him a great feast to celebrate his return (Luke 15:11-32). This is surely the way God feels when someone who returns to the Catholic faith.

Question #43

"Isn't any religion the right one depending on the culture from which you come?" Emily F., 15

A. No. God's truth transcends cultures and time. His

truth is the same in every place and every age.

If religious truth were culturally relative, we would have to accept the human sacrifices of the Aztecs because that sort of thing was acceptable to Aztec culture. This, of course, would not be good. If God reveals a truth, it is true in all places for all time.

Question #44

"What's the difference between Catholic and Christian?" Jonathan S., 14

A. What I believe you are asking is: "What is the difference between Catholicism and Protestant Christianity?"

All Catholics are Christians, but not all Christians are Catholics. A Christian is someone who believes in Jesus Christ as the Son of God and is baptized. A Catholic is a specific kind of Christian — one who also believes the Catholic Church was founded by Christ and who accepts it as possessing the fullness of Christian truth and the means of salvation. This involves three main things: (1) sincerely holding to the Catholic Faith as taught by the Magisterium of the Church (the official teaching body of the Church); (2) accepting the Sacraments of the Catholic Church; and (3) submitting to the teaching authority of the pope and the bishops in communion with him.

There are sincere non-Catholic Christians — Protestant and Orthodox Christians, for instance — who believe many, but not all, of the things we believe as Catholics. Sometimes they may even be more faithful or charitable than many Catholics. That is because the Spirit of Christ is at work in them, too.

The words "Catholic" and "Christian" were once interchangeable. The first Christians called the Church "Catholic" or "universal," to distinguish it from heretical, splinter groups that denied necessary Christian truths. Thus, the early Christians came to be known as Catholics.

Around the year 1,000 A.D. many Christians in the East — in Greece, what is now Turkey — split off from the Catholic Church. They are called Orthodox Christians. They believe many of the same things we do, but also reject important truths such as the pope's authority.

Five hundred years later, a German monk named Martin Luther had some ideas about what true Christianity was. Some of his views were contrary to what Catholics believe Christ intended for His Church. He and his followers broke with the Catholic Church and formed what is now called Lutheranism. Other men and women had ideas of their own and started their own churches, too. Today, there are over 20,000 different Protestant churches.

The Catholic view is that this division and confusion among Christian communities contradicts the will of Jesus. He wants His followers to be one (John 17:11). We believe the unity Christ desires for His followers only exists fully in the Catholic Church.

Question #45

"Why does it seem that Evangelical Protestant teens have a closer relationship with Jesus than Catholic teens?" Amy M., 16

A. Some Evangelical teens do seem to have a closer relationship with Jesus than many Catholic teens. Why? Probably because Evangelical churches stress personal conversion more than individual Catholics typically do. That's unfortunate because the Catholic Church teaches as strongly as Evangelicalism the need for personal conversion.

Furthermore, Evangelicals also emphasize an initial conversion experience when a person steps forward and "accepts Jesus as Savior." This is sometimes known as an "altar call." It can have a profound psychological as well as spiritual effect on a person.

But it's important to recall two things about that sort of thing. First, that human experiences or feelings come and go. What matters is one's continuing commitment to follow Jesus, with or without an "experience."

Jesus says our love for Him is measured by whether we keep His Commandments (John 14:15). If we believe, trust and love Christ by obeying Him, we needn't worry about experiences. A person who claims to have "a personal relationship with Jesus Christ" based on a conversion experience, but who doesn't keep His Commandments, *doesn't* have a close relationship with Christ.

Second, Catholics have an "altar call" every week — the call to receive Jesus in the Holy Eucharist. There is no more "personal relationship" we can have with Christ in this life than to be united with Him in the Holy Eucharist.

Question #46

"Why are Protestant kids into the Bible more than Catholics kids?" Amy M., 13

A. Assuming this is true, that's too bad — not for them — but for Catholic kids. It means only that Catholic kids aren't being Catholic *enough*, for the Catholic Church gave us the Bible and exhorts us to read and study it.

We can see why Protestants would naturally stress the Bible and why Catholics might be tempted to neglect it. The highest authority on earth for the Protestant is the Bible. For the Catholic, the highest authority is the Word of God as it comes to us in the

Bible *and* Sacred Tradition. Plus, God has given us a divinely guided teacher — the Magisterium of the Church — to help us understand Scripture and Tradition. That means we can learn the truths of the Bible without necessarily reading it. The temptation then may be for us to neglect it, which is tragic because God gave the Bible to us to read. To ignore it is to ignore a precious gift. In fact, St. Jerome said "To be ignorant of Scripture is to be ignorant of Christ." As Christians then, we should study Scripture more because of our desire to know more about Christ.

Because Protestant Christians have only the Bible to concern them, they often know it better than most Catholics. (If you only had to study one subject in school, rather than many, imagine how good you'd be in that one subject!) When you know the Bible, you can become enthralled with it. That's why Protestant kids are often more "into the Bible" than Catholics. Fortunately, more Catholics kids are now studying Scripture on a regular basis.

Question #47

"Are we allowed to attend an 'all denominations' Christian retreat?" Adrian A., 15

A. It's not necessarily wrong to attend this type of retreat. However, you should be careful, especially if you're not thoroughly grounded in your Catholic

Faith. It could be confusing or even misleading.

Because retreats are often emotional experiences, you might confuse the "good feelings" you have on retreat with "truth." Simply because something "feels good" doesn't mean it's true. Likewise, just because something doesn't "feel good" doesn't make it wrong or false. Feelings are neither true nor false; they're just feelings.

Also, so called non-denominational or interdenominational events can sometimes be subtly anti-Catholic. Not that the people necessarily intend them to be — they may not even realize it themselves. They just think that being a Christian means believing their way and they don't always appreciate the fact that Catholics hold other ideas.

It would be wise to ask the leaders a few questions before signing up for the retreat. For example, what do they think about the Catholic Church? Do they believe Catholics are Christians, too? Will you be encouraged to participate in a non-Catholic communion service (which you may not do)? Can you leave at any time during the retreat? Are there Catholics among the retreat leaders?

The answers to these questions should help you decide whether or not it would be wise to take part in the retreat.

Question #48

"What is the difference between Catholicism and Mormonism?" Nicole J., 14

A. The basic difference is that Mormonism (also called the Church of Jesus Christ of Latter Day Saints) is a quasi-Christian religion. That means it uses Christian terms like "trinity" and "god" but has very different meanings than traditional Christianity. Sometimes, Mormonism actually contradicts traditional Christian doctrine.

Although Mormons on the whole emphasize the family, morality and patriotism, their religion denies fundamental Christian beliefs, most notably the existence of one *and only one* God. They believe there are many gods made up of flesh and bone like we are. They teach that a "worthy" Mormon man (not women) will become a god and rule over his own planet(s). Mormonism's founder, Joseph Smith, wrote in the book, *Teachings of the Prophet*, "God himself was once as we are now, and is an exalted man, and sits enthroned in the heavens." Catholicism believes there is only one God and He has always existed.

Other Mormon teachings are also contrary to Catholicism. These include the pre-existence of souls, the revelation of the Book of Mormon, the Great Apostasy and a divine curse on black people.

Question #49

"Why don't Jehovah's Witnesses celebrate birthdays?" Anastasia B., 14

A. The Jehovah's Witnesses do not celebrate birthdays because they mistakenly believe the only births celebrated in the Bible are those of wicked men. This isn't true — the birth of Jesus was celebrated by the angels, for example (Luke 2:8-14). Also, John the Baptist's birth was foretold in Scripture and this, of course, would be a moment of great joy. But even if it were true, that still wouldn't mean *we* should not celebrate births.

Jehovah's Witnesses also claim birthday celebrations are pagan in origin and therefore wrong. By that logic, they should not refer to the days of the week or the months of the year by their commonly used names because these are of pagan origin.

Moreover, many of the things we practice today came from paganism, including the exchanging of rings at a wedding, but they have been "Christianized." The Church saw the value in the practice and adopted and blessed it.

Question #50

"Some of my friends are Buddhists. Explain what Buddhism is and what it teaches." Evangeline B., 17

A. Buddhism was founded by Siddhartha Gautama, known as the Buddha (Enlightened One), in southern Nepal in the sixth and fifth centuries B.C. It is an offshoot of Hinduism. The Buddha is said to have achieved "enlightenment" through meditation. He then gathered a community of monks to carry on his teachings.

Buddhism is basically agnostic on the question of God's existence. It is also more of a philosophy than a religion, since it claims no real divine revelation. Buddhism teaches that through meditation and the practice of good religious and moral behavior, one can reach "Nirvana," which is the state of enlightenment. Before reaching Nirvana, one is subjected to repeated reincarnations. The new life is either good or bad depending on your actions or "karma" from past lives.

There are four "noble truths" (doctrines) of the Buddhist. They include: existence is a realm of suffering; desire and the belief in one's importance causes this suffering; reaching Nirvana ends suffering; and Nirvana is attained only by meditation and by following the path of righteousness in action and attitude.

Chapter 7
Catholicism and Society

Question #51

"Why does the Church always disagree with politics?" Tim H., 16

A. The Church doesn't "always disagree with politics," although its teachings contradict some people's political ideas or positions. To understand what this means, we should be clear about what politics is. Politics is the art of governing a society. People sometimes disagree about the best way to govern society. When they do, their disagreements are political.

For the most part, the Magisterium (the teaching office of the Church) doesn't address political issues. Sometimes, however, a moral issue will have political implications. Then the Church does talk about politics, but only because it is obliged to talk about morality.

Consider, for example, the issue of abortion. Because pre-born children are human beings, they have a right to life. Because government is obliged to protect and promote human rights, it is obliged to protect and promote the pre-born child's right to life. When government passes laws or makes legal rulings that deny such a basic human right, it is the duty of the Church to speak out. Not because the Church is concerned with the details of politics or favors one political party or another — it doesn't — but because basic human rights are at stake.

There is a sense, however, in which "the Church" ought to be fully involved with politics: when we mean by "the Church" not merely the Magisterium, but the individual members, especially the laity. Lay men and women are especially called to serve Christ in the world. This means they should apply their Christian moral values to examining and assessing the laws and practices of society. They should try their best to foster laws that uphold God's moral law and do away with those that contradict it. They do this by voting, running for office, communicating with elected officials, peacefully protesting and other means. If elected, they would have an obligation to oppose or inhibit, to the limits of their power, any governmental policy or action in violation of the moral or natural law.

Doing these things will not always be popular, but then again Jesus said his followers wouldn't be popular with the world (Matt. 10:22, Luke 21:17).

Question #52

"What role should the Church play in the world?" Nathan T., 15

A. The Church should teach and sanctify the world, leading it to the One whom God sent as Redeemer and Savior, Jesus.

Its teachings are those given by Jesus to the apostles and their successors, the bishops. The Church sanctifies us by means of the Sacraments, which are channels of grace.

Question #53

"If we are supposed to leave everything and follow God, how come our churches are so exquisite and the people within the church so wealthy?" Andy B., 15

A. The passage of Scripture you refer to concerns the need for everyone who would follow Christ to be detached from possessions. For some of us, according to our vocation, that detachment takes the form of giving up personal ownership of material possessions. For others, personal possessions may be kept and even enjoyed, so long as they are properly used and do not become our "god."

For some people, like the rich young man in St. Mark's Gospel (Mk. 10:17-27), wealth was so important it was really an idol — a false god. To follow

Christ, such people must turn away from their idol, which may sometimes require them to sell everything. But not everyone can or should do that. Parents, for example, can't give away everything they own. How would they fulfill their God-given responsibility to feed and clothe their children? Nevertheless, they should use their possessions with an attitude of willingness to give up everything should it be asked of them. In short, they should serve God, not money (Matt. 6:24).

Regarding the "exquisite" churches and the "wealthy" people who worship in them, several things must be said. First, there's nothing wrong with having beautiful, well-designed churches. Jesus Himself worshipped in the Jerusalem Temple, which was certainly exquisite and expensive. While He condemned the money changers for turning it into a marketplace (Matt. 21:12-13, Mk. 11: 15-17), He never rejected the Temple on the grounds it was ornate or costly.

Also, when Judas objected that expensive oil used to anoint Christ should be sold and the money given to the poor, Jesus didn't agree (John 12:3-8). So, we are allowed to spend money, even large amounts, for things that honor God.

Second, not everyone who attends a beautiful, expensive church is wealthy. A wonderful thing about the great cathedrals and churches is that they are for everyone, poor as well as rich. All are welcome there, where greatness is measured not by how much money one has but by how much love for God and man he has in his heart.

Question #54

"I don't understand why the Church leaders (e.g., pope, bishops) live in luxury when they are the servants of Christ." Michelle P., 15

A. Most bishops don't live in luxury as you suppose. The material resources at their disposal aren't for their private benefit but to carry on the mission of the Church. When a bishop resigns, for example, he doesn't own his bishop's residence anymore than a former president owns the White House when he leaves office.

True, sometimes bishops and even popes of the past have exploited their offices for personal gain. When that occurred, the leaders sinned and deserved rebuke. Nowadays, however, the pope and the bishops seem more conscious that misuse of wealth endangers not only their own souls, but can lead others astray and bring ridicule to the cause of Christ.

In addition, I personally know of one cardinal who used to empty his personal checking account by the end of each year, giving all his money to friends and charities. His aim was to start out each new year with nothing in his personal account. This is a sign of a man who is detached from the material world. I'm sure there are many other Church leaders who who have this sort of detachment from material things.

Even so, people still sometimes accuse our leaders of greed and excess. This is often because critics look upon things like ornate cathedrals or the art treasures of the Vatican as excessive. But bishops don't personally benefit from these things. A cathedral's beauty and the Church's art treasures are for the whole Church — indeed, for humanity. They are a means of honoring God.

Question #55

"How come the Catholic Church is negatively portrayed so much in movies and the news?" Dave G., 14

A. The main reason is because the Catholic Church is the moral leader of the world. It is the voice of reason in an unreasonable age. It stands for truth — and the truth is difficult for many to hear.

Like Jesus, its founder, the Church calls the world to holiness. Most of the world doesn't want to hear this because the Church challenges it to a higher standard of moral living. It tells people that they can't steal, lie, cheat, fornicate, kill and hurt others. And like Jesus, it is persecuted because of its faithfulness to the Gospel.

In fact, I would probably be nervous if the world stopped persecuting the Church. The Church would then be "too worldly." Remember, Jesus said that whoever follows Him faithfully will be persecuted and even hated (Matt. 10:22, Lk. 21:17).

Chapter 8
Catholic Living

Question #56

"What commitments does one need to make when he becomes a Catholic?" Justin M., 15

A. You need to strive to know, love and serve God the Father through His Son Jesus Christ in the power of the Holy Spirit. You commit to being a disciple of Jesus Christ. Since Christ continues to act in the world through the Church with which He is one body, Catholics believe complete discipleship involves adhering to Christ's Word as presented in the teaching of the Catholic Church.

Adhering to the teaching of the Church means assenting to what the Magisterium (the pope and the bishops united with him) teaches as true concerning faith and morals and, by God's grace, living accordingly. Of the Magisterium, Christ said, "Whover listens to you, listens to Me. Whoever rejects you, rejects Me. And whoever rejects Me, rejects the One who sent Me." (Luke 10:16) When the Magisterium teaches, it is Christ teaching.

Receiving Christ's grace through the Sacraments includes accepting Baptism and the Sacraments of initiation (Confirmation, Holy Eucharist), healing (Reconciliation, Anointing of the Sick) and those related to vocation (Holy Matrimony, Holy Orders). The Sacraments are visible, effective signs of Christ's invisible action.

Finally, Christ exercises His pastoral and kingly authority over His followers through the pastors of His Church. Obeying their lawful authority is a way of obeying Christ. Following the pastors includes observing the precepts of the Church. These are commitments to (1) attend Mass on Sundays and Holy Days, (2) confess one's sins at least once a year (if one is conscious of mortal sin); (3) receive Holy Communion during Easter time; (4) observe appointed days of fasting and abstinence; (5) contribute to the support of the Church; and (6) observe the laws of the Church concerning marriage.

These various commitments are all ways our basic Christian commitment to follow Christ are lived out in His Church.

Question #57

"Can a person truly be a Catholic if she is

baptized but does not live a Catholic lifestyle?" Mary B., 13

A. It depends on what you mean by not living a "Catholic lifestyle." Part of a Catholic lifestyle is to believe what the Church teaches. That is really an essential element of being a Catholic. Without faith, it is impossible to be a Catholic, regardless of how "good" a life a person otherwise leads.

On the other hand, we may have faith but not put it into practice — in other words, we can lack charity (or the love of God and neighbor). So long as our faith is genuine and our failure to live it "only" a matter of committing sins, we remain Catholics, albeit poor ones.

We shouldn't count too much on the mere fact that we're Catholics, without regard for whether we're in a state of grace and fellowship with God. One can be a "Catholic" in that sense and still end up separated from God for eternity.

Question #58

"Why is it so important to go to church?" Ryan H., 15

A. Why is it important for a lover to be with his beloved? If we love God, we will want to spend time with Him in the way He wants us to. God wants us to go to church, to give ourselves to Him in worship. And He wants us to do it through His Son's own self-surrender and sacrifice, the Eucharist. All that requires our going to church as God commands.

Another reason for going to church: We receive special graces from worshiping God and from receiving the Eucharist. Going to church can change us and convert our hearts. It can teach us we are not the center of the universe — God is — and He deserves our praise and thanksgiving.

One more point: If we're not worshiping God, we're probably worshiping something else — ourselves, television, a movie star or a sports team. Not going to church doesn't mean we won't worship anything, but that we'll worship the wrong thing.

Question #59

"Is it wrong to practice something like guitar or surfing more than you practice your religion?" Jared K., 15

A. By "practicing your religion," I assume you mean the actual number of minutes or hours in prayer, in study, at church. No, you are not necessarily required to pray more minutes each day than you go surfing. We are physical creatures that need relaxation, laughter, friendship and physical activity. Surfing and guitar playing can actually glorify God if they are done in an excellent manner. We can even practice our faith by doing these types of things if the motive for doing them and the way we do them are correct. They can be offered to God for His glory.

There is not a quota of minutes one has to pray or play each day. Simply keep the following principles in mind: (1) You should strive to want to do God's will more than your own. (2) Keep all activities, including your eventual career, in balance with other aspects of life. These activities should not interfere with family relationships or keeping up your basic religious requirements. (3) Your faith should be an integral part of your life in all activities. People should know you are a person of integrity no matter what activity you are doing. (4) Challenge yourself to grow in prayer and understanding of God. (5) Set some goals that balance your growth in faith with your growth in life's other activities. (e.g., read one religious book for every secular book you read.) Perhaps you could pray 10 extra minutes every day you go surfing. And, (6) stay in a state of grace.

If you keep this type of concern for spiritual growth in mind, you will be on an excellent course towards holiness.

Question #60

"How can I be less hypocritical? I know what Jesus says and what I believe but I often go against these beliefs." Michelle P., 15

A. So does almost everyone in the world. Saints Peter and Paul and every saint in history, except Jesus and Mary, struggled with this very problem. Here are some practical tips that will help you in this struggle: (1) Knowledge is power. If you know your Faith, you'll know more about how to fight against the devil and sin. (2) Read the lives of the saints. They've been where you are now and will inspire you. (3) Live a sacramental life. Go to Mass more than just on Sunday, pray the rosary and go to Confession frequently, especially if you sinned seriously. (4) Ask Jesus for guidance. He will give you the wisdom to know when you are being too hard or easy on yourself.

Question #61

"Why should the pope make our morals and define what is right and wrong?" Rich T., 17

A. He doesn't; God does. The pope simply passes on what Jesus taught.

When a pope is elected to the office, you can bet he is concerned about the awesome task he's been given. He knows the weight of the world will rest on his shoulders every day. This undoubtedly leads him to prayer many times a day.

Defining and passing on faith and morals to a world tainted with original sin is no fun task. Like rebellious children, Catholics and non-Catholics alike often don't want to follow what Christ taught. This makes the pope's job the toughest one in the world.

We should pray for the pope every day so he might persevere in his difficult role as the earthly shepherd for mankind. We should also thank God we have a pope to give us a clear understanding of what is and is not true.

Question #62

"What exactly does 'honor your father and mother' encompass?" Susan K., 17

A. First, it means obey your parents, for they exercise God-given authority over you. It also means to be grateful to your parents for the gift of life, and for you to care for your parents when they can no longer care for themselves.

Children should obey their parents so long as 1) parental wishes aren't contrary to the Catholic Faith; 2) the children live in their parents' home; or 3) until they reach adulthood. After that time, children are still obliged to love and honor their parents, but not necessarily obey them. By this time the children are old enough to make their own decisions.

The Fourth Commandment also applies to more than the parent/child relationship. It calls us to obey lawful superiors, including teachers, older siblings, and those who govern. Again, this assumes one is not directed to act contrary to the Faith.

The Fourth Commandment also places a reciprocal duty on parents and those who exercise other forms of authority. Parents should educate and raise children in the Faith. They should respect their children as persons, disciplining them when necessary and providing for their physical, spiritual, educational and social needs as best they can. In short, parents are obliged to love their children.

Question #63

"What kind of sin is cussing?" Danny N., 14

A. Cursing, also known as cussing or swearing, is a sin against the Second Commandment, "Thou shall not take the name of the Lord thy God in vain." This means that we should never use God's name to express surprise (like, "Oh my G__"!) or anger. Nor should we use words to degrade people, who are made in God's image, for this is a sin against the Fifth Commandment, which obliges us to respect other people as persons made in God's image.

Curse words are like little daggers that pierce the heart of our Lord. When said with full understanding of their sinfulness, with sufficient reflection and with full consent of our wills, they are mortal sins. Fortunately, it is usually a venial sin because most people do not understand the gravity of their action. Here's why this sin can be considered "mortal." In this modern age, we do not understand the glory and majesty of God's name. Several thousand years ago, the Jewish people so honored God's name, Yahweh, they *would not even say it*. They came up with a different name for Him — Adonai. It would have been considered blasphemy to even use God's name correctly, *let alone as a curse word*. To use a name without the proper reverence is to offend the person whose name we are using.

Today, we have become so desensitized to the harsh things the world presents to us we think it is absurd to reverence the name of God. It is not. We need to have reverence for God's name. If we do, our faith will increase. If we do not, we may grow coarse and cold.

Question #64

"Is fighting a sin?" John H., 14

A. It depends. If fighting is done out of aggression, especially if one seeks to seriously injure another person, then it is a grave sin against the Fifth Commandment, "You shall not kill." That Commandment refers not merely to killing, but any attempt to unjustly harm another person.

Jesus taught that we shouldn't try to "get even" for attacks on ourselves, even physical attacks, so long as they involve only ourselves and cause no serious harm. That's really what he meant by "Turn the other cheek (Matt. 5:39, Lk. 6:29)."

However, if attacks on others are also involved or there is a chance of injury to oneself, then the Commandment "Thou shalt not kill" does not apply to us. We can protect ourselves and are obliged to protect others as best we can. But, we are to use only as much force as necessary to stop an aggressor.

"Turn the other cheek" means we shouldn't start fights, and we should forgive offenses. It doesn't mean, however, we have to be beaten up by a cruel aggressor.

Question #65

"Is it a sin to kill animals?" Brant W., 15

A. Animals can justly be used for food, clothing, medical testing and, even, in moderation, for sports. Nevertheless, we should avoid cruelty to animals and unnecessary infliction of pain.

Scripture reveals it was in God's plan that man subdue and have dominion over the earth (Gen. 1:28). However, this position of dominion can be taken to an extreme. We are not allowed to indiscriminately abuse or kill animals for pleasure. The *Catechism* says this dominion is "not an arbitrary or destructive domination" (CCC #373).

While there is nothing wrong with working to prevent cruelty to animals, we should work all the harder to defend human rights, especially for the most vulnerable among us such as pre-born babies, the infirmed, and the poor.

Question #66

"What can you do to help set your friend straight without losing the friendship?" Kelly A., 15

A. The greatest thing you can do for a friend is to tell him or her the truth in love. You are not really a friend if you let that person continue living a sinful life. This is "false compassion." We think we are being nice by not saying anything, but we may be helping the person risk losing his or her soul.

The book of Genesis says we *are* our brother's keeper (Gen. 4:9). We *are* responsible for the action of others to a certain degree. We could be committing a sin of omission if we do not say something.

I would recommend that you pray, ask other responsible people like a priest or parent for guidance and then say something to your friend with heartfelt love and compassion. In the end, that person may appreciate it. Be sure to keep your friend in your prayers after you deliver the message.

Question #67

"How can I convince friends who go to church once or twice a month or just on holi-

days why they need to go regularly?" Clare H., 14

A. It sounds as if they don't realize what the heart of their professed Faith is — a relationship of love with Jesus Christ. Perhaps you should work on that. Evangelize them by pointing them to Christ. The best way to do that isn't simply by what you say, but also what you do. Your love for Christ should be evident by how you live. If you're a hypocrite, your friends may see this as proof that going to Mass makes no difference.

As to why they should go to Mass regularly, tell them they should do this as an expression of their love for Christ. This love of Christ means (1) we want to receive Him in the Eucharist and (2) we will obey Him. Jesus says if we love Him, we will keep His Commandments (John 14:15). Conversely, if we don't keep His Commandments, can we really say we love Him?

Jesus wants us to gather for corporate worship on Sundays. That is how Christians fulfill the Commandment, "Keep holy the Lord's Day."

Remind your friend that God gives us 24 hours each day. He gives seven days each week. That's 168 hours a week. We spend about 56 hours sleeping and 56 hours working or in school. That leaves

56 hours for enjoyment, etc. If we can't give God one or two hours out of that 56, there's simply *no way* we can say we love Him. And, if you do not love or serve Him in this life, you seriously risk not being with Him in the next.

Question #68

"What can we do to promote more Catholic living to nominal Catholics?" Therese J., 15

A. Live the Faith yourself with conviction. Don't be "lukewarm." Also have the courage to explain the practical reasons for living the Faith. Explain how the Church's moral teachings protect us from physical and spiritual harm.

If this doesn't work, you may have to verbally "hit them between the eyes" with the tough message offered by Scripture. Tell them what Jesus says about those who are lukewarm. In the book of Revelation, Jesus says: "So, because you are lukewarm, neither hot nor cold, I will spit you out of my mouth." (Rev. 3:16). Other translations have used the phrase "vomit you out of my mouth." Tell them if they die in a state of apathy towards God, they seriously risk an eternity *without* the One they ignored in life.

Question #69

"Many of my friends and even strangers try to question my Faith. I have tried to debate

with them, but you can't argue with people who have their minds set. What do you suggest I say in reply?" Jessica N., 14

A. Yes you can argue with people who have their minds set. You simply have to come up with better arguments. You first need to ask them if they're *really* interested in discussing or are they debating simply for the sake of debating. If they are interested in discussing the issues, you then need to thoroughly know their positions. Be a good listener and be charitable. Don't be too defensive.

If you don't have an answer, be frank and tell them so. But, then tell them you will get back to them *and then do so.* Stay on one issue at a time. Don't let the person jump from issue to issue. Write down what you've resolved so you don't have to re-address the same issues again.

Pray that the Holy Spirit will guide you and that you'll remain humble. Be sure to pray that the person(s) receives the gift of faith. Faith is a gift. Believing in the Catholic Church is a gift. All the arguments in the world won't convince people *without God's grace.* So, pray to God that they receive this grace. And pray that your friends respond.

Question #70

"How can youth leaders get Catholic teens

more excited about God in their youth groups or Church?" Amy M., 16

A. As a former youth minister I worked with many kids who could be classified as "lukewarm." They didn't care too much about religion. They were bored in religious education classes. They were probably apathetic because they were not more convinced about the truths of the Faith.

I recommend trying to get them fully convinced about *just one issue*, perhaps abortion. After they come to see that truth exists and that it is vitally important, you can then introduce them to other truths. You can convince them that "objective truth" exists and that we need to act on this truth. They will start to see the ridiculousness of the "live and let live" mentality. How can one let an Adolf Hitler "do his own thing?" How can one sit by as millions of babies are killed each year in abortion? An energetic, even mildly confrontational faith will excite them. Then you can introduce them to a deeper sacramental and contemplative approach to the Faith.

Question #71

"Is it okay for Catholics to listen to non-Christian music?" Amy M., 16

A. Sure, as long as it is done in moderation and if the music does not contain lyrics that are sexually explicit or overly violent or cruel. Although people say, "I don't listen to the lyrics, I just like the music," the message still gets through. There's no way we can constantly guard against the influence the media has on us. Therefore, you should be cautious.

Listening to music that contains lyrics contrary to the Christian Faith may lead one to sin. It may also desensitize you. A good rule of thumb when deciding on whether certain music is not spiritually dangerous is to ask, "Would Jesus listen to this music for relaxation?" If the answer is "no," then you should also stay away.

Question #72

"How does one become a saint?" Thang P., 19

A. One becomes a saint by doing the will of God, which is another way of saying loving God above everything else.

This type of life includes living a sacramental life and practicing the virtues, especially humility. A sacramental life should include frequent Mass (at least on Sunday, if not a few times each week), frequent Confession (perhaps once a month and immediately after serious sin) and daily prayer, including the rosary.

A virtuous life includes striving for perfection in faith, hope and charity. Faith is believing in things not fully seen; hope is trusting in the promises of our

Lord; and charity is the act of loving others. Continual striving for perfection in these areas, along with living a sacramental life, will put you on course for sainthood.

You may also consider meeting regularly with a spiritual director. Meeting with an older brother or sister in the Faith such as a priest or religious sister will help you learn from another's experiences and wisdom. In addition, by working with the same person on a regular basis, he or she will get to know you, your personality, your struggles and your strengths. You should then receive better and more specific recommendations on how to strengthen your walk with the Lord.

Chapter 9
Catholic Beliefs and Practices

Question #73

"In Baptism, is the baby made a friend of God?" Ravi D., 17

A. Yes. Like circumcision in the Old Testament, Baptism makes the baby a member of the family of God. However, Baptism is more powerful than circumcision because it is built on a better foundation — Jesus Christ and the New Covenant He established.

Baptism does at least three things for the one being baptized: (1) It unites us to Jesus Christ. (2) It gives supernatural life to a soul that was previously dead through original or actual sin by infusing sanctifying grace. (Sanctifying grace is necessary for salvation.) In adults, Baptism also removes actual sins that were committed before Baptism. (3) It makes the child or adult a member of the Church.

Question #74

"I thought we receive the Holy Spirit in Con-

firmation, yet I heard we also receive Him in Baptism. How can we receive what we already have? Do we just receive a blessing in Baptism?" Nicholas, 14

A. You receive the Holy Spirit first in Baptism and then again in a special way at Confirmation. At Baptism, the Holy Spirit is sent to wash away original sin and bring your soul to a state of grace. Prior to Baptism, the soul of the person is tainted with the effects of original sin, which makes us unfit for eternal life. At Baptism, we become members of the Church.

In Confirmation, we receive different graces which prepare us to be adult Christians. We receive a special grace which enables us to more boldly live and profess our Faith. At Confirmation, we are enrolled as soldiers in the Church's spiritual army. It also strengthens the graces and gifts we received at Baptism. The grace in Confirmation is more "tailor made" for this next stage of our life of Faith.

Question #75

"If a baby is aborted and was never baptized, will it go to heaven?" Ravi D., 17

A. We don't know for sure. The *Catechism of the Catholic Church* says the following: "As regards children who have died without Baptism, the Church can only entrust them to the mercy of God, as she does in her funeral rites for them. Indeed, the great mercy of God, who desires that all men should be saved, and Jesus' tenderness toward children which caused him to say: 'Let the children come to me, do not hinder them' (Mk. 10:14), allow us to hope that there is a way of salvation for children who have died without Baptism" (CCC #1260).

Question #76

"Why do you have to go to Confession? Why can't we just go to God for forgiveness?" Genny C., 13

A. Because God wants to reach us through the Church, the community of believers. He wants us to be a family. So He gave us spiritual fathers in the priesthood. The priests have the authority to administer His forgiveness to us. "Whose sins you forgive, they are forgiven. Whose sins you retain, they are retained," Jesus told the apostles (John 20:21-23).

Actually, we *can* go "directly" to God, but also through His Church. God sees the two as linked. Our sin, even if we suppose it is only "against God," robs our fellow believers of something — of our being in communion with God and them. It diminishes the power of the Church because sin cuts us off from full communion together in the Holy Spirit. We become like a dead limb, just barely hanging on. Dead limbs can be harmful to the tree.

The Church, you see, is like a body. When one member suffers, the whole body suffers. To be reconciled, we must not only repent before God, we must also have reconciliation with the Church. That's the way God wants it.

Remember what Jesus said we must do if we're making an offering to God and we recall that someone has a grievance against us? He said we should be reconciled with our brother first, then make our offering to God (Matt. 5:21-26). Why is that? Because reconciliation with God and with His people are tied together.

God also gave us confession because it is humbling. Humility is the first step towards true repentance. Because pride is the root of all sin, an act of humility such as confessing to a priest will help push out the pride in our lives. In addition, the priest can keep us more objective about our sins. The priest can also give you a concrete "plan of action" to avoid sin in the future. If we go directly to God in the privacy of our own home, we can deceive ourselves. We can either be too harsh or lenient.

Question #77

"If God knows everything we do, then how come we have to go to Confession?" Amber H., 19

A. We go to Confession to say "I'm sorry" for our

sins, not to tell God something He doesn't already know. You may know your younger brother broke your CD player, but wouldn't it be aggravating if he knew you knew, but still didn't say "I'm sorry." It would be a double smack in the face.

In addition to saying "sorry" to God, Confession also restores us to the Church. There is no such thing as a private sin. In some way, every sin affects the world in a negative manner. There is always a ripple effect.

Also, when a Catholic accepts and takes advantage of the Sacrament of Penance, he builds up the body of Christ. He is implicitly saying, "I believe in the Sacrament and you should, too." This affirmation of the Sacrament can lead others to live a sacramental life.

Question #78

"Doesn't God forgive you no matter what? Therefore, isn't Confession unnecessary?" Emily F., 15

A. What you're asking is, "Doesn't God just 'look the other way' when we sin?" Or, if He really loves us, why does He let our sins get in the way of our relationship with Him? Why does He demand repentance first? Why can't He forgive us unconditionally?

The answer is that forgiveness, by its very nature,

requires acceptance on the part of the one forgiven in order to be complete. The goal of forgiveness is reconciliation. The person who admits no fault can accept no forgiveness for it and cannot be reconciled with the one he has offended by his action.

God cannot just "ignore" our sin because He is holy. Also, because sin hurts us, God won't allow us to be hurt unnecessarily. He loves us too much to leave us in our sin. The only way out is repentance.

Furthermore, sin itself keeps us from God, who is our ultimate happiness, so long as we are unrepentant. If we think of sin as merely breaking the rules, especially rules seen as arbitrarily laid down by God, then it is hard to understand why God can't just "look the other way." But if sin is understood as preferring some lesser good (*something* else or *someone* else, including ourselves) to God, the supreme Good, then God's love for us demands that He set us straight. He requires us to turn back to Him — for our sake, not His. God wants us to turn our hearts from the lesser good to Himself, our supreme Good.

The Sacrament of Confession is the normal means God has established for us to come back to Him if we sin seriously after Baptism. Confession is an expression of God's love for us, for He knows our hearts and our need to confess.

Question #79

"Does Confession give people the idea that its all right to sin as long as you're sorry later?" Emily F., 15

A. There's no reason it should. People who think that way are mistaken, either due to ignorance or choice.

Confession means God's forgiveness is available if we repent, not that it's okay to sin so long as you repent. Would you intentionally break your arm because you knew a doctor could fix it later?

We should never sin thinking we needn't worry because God will forgive us later. That itself is the sin of presumption, presuming God's mercy regardless of His Commandments.

Sin involves turning our backs on God in some way. We should never try to "use" God by turning away from Him *now* assuming that *later* we shall turn back to Him. Why? First, because that casts doubt about the sincerity of our later repentance. True repentance involves genuine sorrow for having sinned and the willingness never to do it again. How likely is it that we shall truly be repentant — sorry for having sinned to begin with — if all along we thought to ourselves that we would enjoy sin now and repent later?

Second, how do we know that "later" will ever come? Death could come at any time. What if it comes before you are sorry or repentant?

It is very dangerous to live a life of serious and frequent sin. Sin is very "attractive" (although superficial) and can be quite addictive. One may get caught up in a certain way of living without even knowing the magnitude of the problem. One could get hooked on a particular sin and not know how enslaved he or she really is to that sin. We should be constantly on guard against sin.

Question #80

"Is a priest necessary for forgiveness in Confession or will God forgive you as soon as you are sorry for the sin?" Ravi D., 17

A. When we sin seriously, we lose sanctifying grace and cut ourselves off from God. When this happens, God gives us "actual grace" to work on our conscience to bring us back to Him. If we realize our sin at this point and repent — have perfect contrition for our sins, which means supernaturally loving God above all things for His sake — then we're on our way back home. If we should die at that point, our sins would be forgiven. But otherwise, we are still obliged to confess our sins to a priest.

Why? Because God has willed that we use the Sacrament of Confession, even if we have already made an act of perfect contrition. Sin requires reconciliation with the Church as well as with God as we have seen. An act of perfect contrition may reconcile us with God, but He still expects us to seek reconciliation with the Church. Furthermore, if we are truly reconciled with God through perfect contrition, we will implicitly want to do His will, which includes going to Confession as soon as we can.

Question #81

"Does God forgive us even when we don't forgive and forget ourselves?" Erinn T., 16

A. Yes, assuming we went to Confession or made an act of perfect contrition (if we were in an emergency situation). There are a few reasons why people don't "forgive themselves" after Confession. Some people suffer from scrupulosity, which is a disease of the soul where the person confessing never "feels" forgiven. This can often be remedied by spiritual or secular counseling. Some others simply need more catechetical instruction on the power of the Sacrament and how God completely blots out our sin when we seek forgiveness.

It's important to remember the Sacraments transmit God's saving grace whether we "feel" it or not. As long as we truly have contrition for (and repent of) our sins, God will forgive us.

Question #82

"Can you be forgiven for committing murder?" Tom S., 14

A. Yes, if one is truly sorry. The only unforgiveable sin is final impenitence, which is a rejection of God even up to death. This is referred to in Scripture as the "unforgivable sin" against the Holy Spirit (Luke 12:10).

Question #83

"Is it a sin to go to Communion after having been sexually active with someone if you ask God for forgiveness in your heart (and not go to Confession)? Will you go to hell for this?" Name and age withheld

A. To begin, I assume you are not married to the person with whom you are sexually active.

It is a sin to go to Communion if you have serious sin on your soul and have not asked for forgiveness from God through the ordinary means He established — Confession to a priest.

St. Paul says very clearly in his letter to the Corinthian Catholics that a person who "eats the bread and drinks the cup of the Lord unworthily will have to answer for the body and blood of the Lord" (1 Cor. 11:27). To someone who lives in the Middle East, the phrase "answer for the body and blood of the Lord" means that a person is guilty of killing the Lord.

St. Paul goes on to say that anyone "who eats and drinks without discerning the body (of the Lord), eats and drinks judgement upon himself" (1 Cor. 11:29). As you see, St. Paul is very serious about the need to be in a state of grace when you receive the Eucharist.

If you commit a serious sin, sexual or otherwise, you should ask God for forgiveness immediately. But you should also make every reasonable effort to go to Confession before attending Mass. If you have not received the Sacrament of Reconciliation, you should refrain from receiving the Eucharist until you have done so.

You should still attend Mass on Sundays and participate in other aspects of the liturgy, but not receive the Eucharist. You can express repentance by worshipping Him at Mass, taking part in the penitential rite and listening to His Word proclaimed in the readings.

Furthermore, you should seek "spiritual communion" with Jesus at Mass. This is a form of communion with Him through prayer alone, when one cannot approach and receive Jesus in the Eucharist. You should say a prayer like this: "Jesus, I cannot receive You today, but I wish You to dwell in me."

As for whether you'll go to hell, that depends on whether you are in God's friendship when you die. The Bible makes it clear that receiving Communion unworthily is not a small matter. It is a serious sin: sacrilege. Also, we should not presume we can sin habitually and yet still get to heaven.

Question #84

"How do you determine if you can receive Communion or not?" Angela R., 15

A. By examining your conscience to determine, as best as you can, whether you are in a state of grace — whether you have committed any mortal sins that have not been confessed. If you are in a state of grace, you can and should receive the Eucharist. If you are not, you should not receive it. To do so would be the sin of sacrilege.

As you grow in the spiritual life, you will generally find it easier to determine whether you have committed any mortal sins. In the meantime, here is a quick lesson on what constitutes a mortal sin.

A mortal sin is a grievous offense against God that deprives the sinner of sanctifying grace, which is the supernatural life of the soul. It also makes the person an enemy of God, takes away all the merits of one's good actions and deprives one of the sanctifying grace necessary for salvation. To commit a mortal (or deadly) sin, there are three conditions that must be present: (1) the thought, word, action or omission must be seriously wrong or considered seriously wrong, (2) the sinner needs to know it is seriously wrong, and (3) the sinner must give full consent of the will in choosing the sin.

I've enclosed an "Examination of Conscience" at the end of the book. Cut it out or photocopy it and keep it with you. This will help you examine your conscience to determine whether you have committed a serious offense against God. As you become more sensitive to God's laws (which comes from prayer, study and frequent reception of the Sacraments), you will know almost immediately when you have committed a serious offense.

Question #85

"At Mass, how is the bread and wine God's body and blood? When I see the bread, I don't see flesh or skin. Also, the wine is not thick enough to be blood." John D., 14

A. You're right that in the Eucharist we don't see the flesh and blood of Christ in their natural forms. That's because the Eucharist is a *sacrament*, which means it's a *sign*. The *sign* can be discerned (seen, heard, felt, tasted or touched), but not Christ's actual flesh. So, we have to have faith in the invisible reality.

For example, you can't see your sins being forgiven in Baptism. All you see is water being poured on you (and all you "feel" is wet). Yet, we really and truly have our sins removed with Baptism. We can discern (feel) the water. We have to have faith to believe that the forgiveness of sins actually took place.

In the case of the Eucharist, all we see are the appearances of bread and wine, rather than the invisible reality, which is Christ's glorified body and blood (as well as His soul and divinity).

Things we encounter have "substance" and "accidents." "Substance" refers to the thing itself that exists *in itself* rather than as an *aspect* of something *else.* A tree, a car, a human being are "substances" in this sense. But these things also have certain qualities or characteristics that don't exist on their own but *in* them.

Think of it this way: A tree may have green leaves or brown. A car may be red or green. A human may be tall or short, etc. These characteristics are real, but they don't exist on their own; they exist as attributes of *other* things. We never, for instance, run into "redness" or "tallness." These qualities exist, but only in other things that are red or tall — that car or that boy. We call such qualities *the accidents* (in technical language, not in the ordinary sense of the word, i.e., something unintended).

Another example: a house is substance; the paint adhering to the house is an accident. If we paint the house another color, we've changed the accident but kept the substance. The house is still a house. It doesn't change to a tree or a car.

Now the Eucharist is like that; it has both substance and accidents. When the priest consecrates the Eucharist, the accidents of bread and wine remain while their substance is changed into the body and blood of Christ. It looks like bread and tastes like bread, but has really and truly changed to the Body and Blood of Christ.

Ordinarily, a change of substance would mean a change in accidents, for the accidents of a thing usually go along with the substance. But in the Eucharist we do not see a change in accidents because God maintains the accidents of bread and wine (the color, shape, taste, smell, etc.) despite changing their substance to that of the Body and Blood of Christ.

Why does God retain the accidents of bread and wine? First, to remind us that Christ is the source of our spiritual, as well as physical, life using the appearance of bread and wine, which help give us physical life. (God often links the physical and spiritual together like that.) Second, to become one with us physically (as we eat the Eucharistic elements) as a means of joining with us spiritually — communion. (He can do that with the accidents of bread and wine, which can be taken into our bodies to become part of us.) Third, to link the Eucharist to His covenant with the Jewish people, for the elements of bread and wine are taken from the Passover meal of the Hebrews. Fourth, to link the Eucharist with every meal, where when the food is blessed, we acknowledge God as Lord of our lives and of creation. The Eucharist is the supreme act of acknowledgment, for in it we offer God's supreme gift to us, Jesus, back to Him. And with the Eucharist, we also offer ourselves to God.

Question #86

"Do any other Christian faiths have communion?" Elisabeth G., 18

A. Most Christian churches have some form of communion. But, excluding a few rare exceptions, only the Eastern Orthodox have the same Eucharist as the Roman Catholic Church — the Body and Blood of Christ made present under the "appearances" of bread and wine. Like Catholic priests, Orthodox priests have apostolic succession and valid priestly orders, so they are able to change bread and wine into the Body and Blood of Christ.

Most Anglicans (and their American counterparts, Episcopalians) and Lutherans believe in a form of the Real Presence — that Jesus' body and blood are present *along with* the "substance" of bread and wine — a view the Catholic Church rejects. Most Evangelical or Fundamentalist Protestants deny any form of "Real Presence" of Jesus in Communion. They teach that Jesus is either only "spiritually" present, as He is at other times when Christians gather, or symbolically present, with the bread and wine simply *representing* Him. The Catholic Church also rejects these views as incomplete at best.

Question #87

"Is Christ more present in the Eucharist than He is in society?" Ravi D. 17

A. First we should be clear how Jesus is present in society. Jesus is present in society because He is God, and God is everywhere and in everything by His power, essence and knowledge. Jesus is also present in society because each person is made in God's image and Jesus is the supreme embodiment of that image. That is why He could say of the poor: "Whatever you do to the least of these...you do to me" (Matt. 25:40). And Jesus is also present in society through His Holy Spirit calling all to communion with the Father in the Church. Finally, Christ is present in society insofar as He is in the Church herself: in His Word, in His people, in His priests, and above all, in the Holy Eucharist.

In the Eucharist, however, Christ is present in an even more profound way than how He is present in society. His Body, Blood, Soul and Divinity are present. Whereas, in society, He's present in a purely spiritual manner. Though the Eucharistic Presence of Christ is, in a sense, concealed by the appearances of bread and wine, Jesus Christ is really, truly and substantially present there. This is why we genuflect before the tabernacle at church — Christ is present there uniquely. This is why we show reverence when approaching Holy Communion. This is why we have Eucharistic adoration — worshipping the Eucharistic Christ as God. And this is why we kneel at the consecration — bending our knees before the God who made us.

How great a mystery it is that in the Eucharist, the Creator, Savior and Lord of the universe comes to us, His mere creatures, in the form of food for our bodies, though He is truly food for our souls as well.

Question #88

"What is Confirmation?" Tara O., 14

A. Confirmation is one of the three Sacraments of initiation; the others are Baptism and the Holy Eucharist. These Sacraments make us part of — or more fully part of — Christ's Church. Confirmation is the Sacrament by which the Holy Spirit comes to us in a radical way after Baptism, to strengthen us ("confirmation" means "strengthening"), to increase and deepen the grace of our Baptism and to make us "soldiers for Christ." Through the Sacrament of Confirmation, we are specially equipped to spread and defend the Faith by word and deed, as witnesses of Jesus.

The bishop usually confers the Sacrament, though priests can also do so with permission. The minister of the Sacrament extends his hands over those who wish to be confirmed, prays over them and anoints them with holy oil. Oil is used because it is a symbol of strength. In ancient times, athletes used to use oil to limber up their muscles to prepare for the contest. In spiritual terms, we are being prepared for the spiritual contest ahead of us.

All too often, young people are apathetic to Confirmation. Perhaps it's because of poor catechetical instruction or because they are overstimulated with television, movies and popular culture. Either way, they need to know that the things of God are not to be taken lightly. I suspect if we get to heaven, we will see the crucial role our Confirmation played in bringing us to eternal peace and happiness with God.

Question #89

"Why did God make marriage one of the seven Sacraments?" Joel O., 13

A. Christ gave us the Sacraments as ordinary means of receiving His grace. He used commonplace things like water (for Baptism), oil (for Confirmation and Anointing of the Sick) or bread and wine (the Holy

Eucharist) so the Sacraments would be readily available to us and, more importantly, as special ways of making holy these ordinary, earthly things. Marriage is one of those ordinary things that Christ elevated to the supernatural level and made a means of grace.

Why marriage is important should be obvious. It provides a place for children to come into being with the irreplaceable love only two parents, committed to one another as well as their children, can give.

Question #90

"What is considered a valid Catholic marriage in the eyes of the Catholic Church? Does the ceremony need to be officiated by a priest?" Susan K., 17

A. There are several components that need to be present in order for a marriage to be valid. They are "capacity," "consent" and "form." If one of these is missing, for either of the two parties, the marriage is not valid. Let me explain each:

"Capacity" is the question of whether the two are *able* to get married. Impediments that would go against capacity include one's age or whether the person is already married.

"Consent" is the question of whether the two actually *mean* the words they are saying in the ceremony. If someone is planning not to allow the children to be raised Catholic or is planning to "try out" marriage to see if it works, they are not fully consenting and the marriage would probably be invalid. Psychological immaturity or a gross misunderstanding of the nature of marriage are also conditions that may hinder one's valid consent. Approximately two-thirds of all annulments in recent years have been granted because of a lack of consent on the part of at least one of the two parties.

"Form" is the question of *how* the marriage is contracted. A Catholic marriage before a justice of the peace is not valid. A marriage without the official representative of the Church *and* two witnesses would not be valid.

There is a book called *100 Answers to Your Questions on Annulments* by Dr. Edward Peters, a canon and civil lawyer, which offers clear answers on marriage and annulments. If you want more specifics, refer to that book. I've listed it in the "Resources" section in the back of this book.

Question #91

"Does the Church advise against marrying a non-Catholic?" Helen M., 17

A. The Church encourages marriages between Catholics and warns against the added difficulties which can accompany mixed marriages (marriages between a Catholic and a baptized non-Catholic) and what are called marriages with disparity of cult (marriages between a Catholic and a non-baptized person).

There are serious dangers in a mixed marriage. The couple risks bringing the issues of Christian disunity into their marriage and family life. Catholics and non-Catholic Christians often have profound differences on matters of doctrine, morality, sacramental worship and church practice that can pose grave problems, especially with respect to raising children and their religious formation. Problems are even more severe where Catholics and non-Christians marry.

Here's another reason: When someone marries a non-Catholic, the *Catholic* might have a more difficult time practicing his or her Faith. The two people are not taking advantage of the most valuable marital resources available: God and His Church. When questions of morality, finances, the raising of children or some other important issues arise, the spouses may approach the problem from different perspectives. This can even happen to two Protestant Christians who worship in different denominations.

Because the Church has 2,000 years of collective wisdom on this topic, it knows the challenges and sacrifices that couples face. When both parties have devotion to the Eucharist or Our Lady, and take advantage of frequent Confession, they are well equipped to handle problems due to the special grace that comes their way.

Catholics need the express permission of Church authorities to marry lawfully a non-Catholic Christian and the same to validly marry a non-Christian. For more information, you should speak to your pastor.

Question #92

"Can a Catholic be married to a Protestant without the Protestant converting first? If so, how?" Mary B., 13

A. Yes. Although it would most likely help the marriage if the Protestant did embrace the Faith, it is not mandatory. Some theologians may even say it would be better to marry a fervent Protestant (as long as he or she is not anti-Catholic) than a nominal Catholic. However, your best bet in almost all cases is find someone with whom you share a deep Catholic Faith.

If a Catholic marries a non-Catholic, baptized Christian, the two need to follow the laws of the Church regarding marriage. One of these laws is the commitment to raise the kids Catholic.

Question #93

"Why can't people get divorces in the Catholic Church?" Andy D., 13

A. Divorce is a matter of civil law, not the law of

God. A validly married couple who divorce may think their action has ended their marriage before God or in the eyes of the Church, but that's not true. They're still married.

Divorce must be distinguished from an annulment, which is a declaration that what *appeared* to be a marriage was not in fact a true marriage, because it lacked some necessary element.

Divorce and remarriage violate natural and divine laws. They break the covenant to which the spouses freely consented, namely to live with each other until the death of one of the spouses. Divorce also introduces disorder into the family and society as a whole. This can bring great harm to one or both of the spouses and certainly the children.

The Sacrament of Matrimony expresses the relationship between Christ and His Church. Christ is no bigamist — He is "Bridegroom" of only one "Bride," the Church. So too in marriage. Remarriage after divorce is just another form of polygamy (having more than one spouse), only the spouses come after each other instead of all at once.

Question #94

"When and why can one get an annulment?" Katie V., 14

A. Annulments are granted by Church authority when it is determined that no valid marriage existed between a couple because of lack of some necessary element for a marriage to occur, on the part of one or both parties: a lack of true consent, the capacity to marry or proper form.

Question #95

"If a women is abused by her husband, could she get an annulment?" Gabriela S., 17

A. Only if the "marriage" was not valid to begin with. Spousal abuse *may* be an indicator of other problems which could have been present when the marriage was contracted that invalidated it, but this is by no means certain.

It is also possible that someone in a valid marriage later chose to become abusive.

In an abusive situation where the marriage is valid, an annulment is not possible. A spiritual advisor or counselor such as a priest may recommend a temporary or even indefinite separation because of the danger to one or both of the involved parties, but the hope is that this situation is temporary. If it ends up being an extended situation, neither of the parties can remarry.

Again, the abuse may be a symptom of some deeper

problem. This deeper problem may offer some reason to render the marriage invalid. If not, then the
abused party should offer up his or her sufferings
with the sufferings of Christ. Picking up this heavy
cross will be difficult, but it can be the path to eternal life.

Question #96
"Is everything we do a sin?" John H., 14

A. Certainly not. Only actions which are seriously
wrong and then freely chosen are considered sins.
Also, unless we have given the matter sufficient reflection and full consent of our will, we are not necessarily culpable (blameworthy) even if what we do
is wrong in itself.

God created us with free will. Because of original
sin we have an *inclination* towards sin, but are not
absolutely drawn to it like a powerful magnet is
drawn to metal. Nor are we ever forced into sin by
Satan. Sin is ultimately our choice. By relying on
God's grace and practicing the virtues, we *can* avoid
sin and lead a virtuous life.

Learning more about your Faith, including the Commandments and Beatitudes, participating in the Mass
and reading the Bible will help you develop a deeper
understanding of what sin is and is not.

Question #97
"What does the Catholic Church consider a sin?" Bob K., 15

A. The word sin is used in many different senses. The main definition refers to a thought, word, action or omission contrary to God's moral law. It amounts to saying "no" to God. It is a great evil because it deprives God of the honor due Him and the respect His laws require.

The Church speaks of original sin and actual sin. Original sin is not, strictly speaking, sin — at least not for us. It is the loss of grace human beings would otherwise come into existence with had our original parents not sinned against God. Because of original sin, we inherit death, a darkened intellect, a weakened will to resist evil and corruptibility, including vulnerability to sickness and old age. Actual sin, on the other hand, refers to sin *we* actually commit.

Specific sins are listed in the Ten Commandments. Although each Commandment addresses a specific sin, there are related sins under each of the ten. For example, the Fifth Commandment is "Thou shalt not kill." In addition to the obvious prohibition against murder, this also means other things like revenge, reckless driving, giving bad example by your actions, drunkenness and sins against human life.

Another example is the Seventh Commandment,

"Thou Shalt Not Steal." In addition to obvious things like taking money from someone without their knowing it, this Commandment also covers things like accepting bribes, cheating on your taxes or damaging someone's property.

The more you learn the Faith, the more you will come to see what is and is not sinful. Also, the more you go to Confession, the more sensitive your soul becomes to right and wrong. I recommend reading the Beatitudes found in St. Matthew's Gospel. You may also want to look at the Examination of Conscience at the end of this book.

Question #98

"What are mortal sins and what makes them different from venial sins?" Jared K., 15

A. *Mortal sin* is a serious offense against God that deprives the soul of sanctifying grace, which is necessary for salvation. It also takes away all merit of our previous good actions and separates us from God. This grace and merit can be restored once we are reconciled to God. A sin is mortal when it involves a serious matter (such as one of the Commandments), when we sufficiently reflect on its seriousness, and when we choose to do it anyway by giving the full consent of our wills. With mortal sin, we lose the virtue of charity (love). We may retain the other two theological virtues of faith and hope, but these are not sufficient by themselves for salvation.

Mortal sins are like the nails that were driven into Jesus' hands and feet. It is precisely because of these sins (past, present and future) that He died on the cross.

Venial sin is a less serious offense against God that does not cause us to lose sanctifying grace. Strictly speaking, we do not have to go to Confession for venial sins, although it is certainly helpful to our spiritual development to confess them when we think of them. A sin is venial when it is not seriously wrong or, if seriously wrong, it is done with less than full knowledge or full consent. Venial sin harms us by making us less fervent to serve God.

If mortal sin is death to the soul, then venial sin should be considered a wound to the soul. If left unattended, venial sin can weaken us and make us susceptible to more serious sins.

Question #99

"What kind of sins prevent you from entering the gates of heaven?" Clare H., 14

A. Any mortal sins which a person does not repent of before death will keep him from heaven. Mortal sin is when we reject God's love or truth by choosing something incompatible with the love of God.

Since heaven is the eternal presence of God and hell the eternal absence of God, the person who sins mortally and dies alienated from God will get what he wants — an eternity without God, but it is to that person's everlasting sorrow.

Question #100

"If someone tells you something is a sin and you disagree with it, is it a sin?" Katie V., 14

A. It depends on who the "someone" is. If God says something is a sin, it's a sin. If the Magisterium of the Church (the pope and the other bishops united with him) teach something is a sin (contrary to God's law), then it's a sin. This is because Jesus promised the Magisterium special guidance to teach about matters of right and wrong without error (Matt. 16:18, Matt. 28:20, Mk. 16:16, Lk. 10:16, 1 Tim. 3:15). Otherwise, just because someone says something is wrong doesn't make it so, although we should be willing to consider the advice of wiser men and women, especially parents, in such matters.

A real danger today is to think sin is merely a matter of opinion. It is not. If something is a sin, it's a sin regardless of what you or I think about it. True, if we are in genuine ignorance, we may not be held accountable for a sinful action. But that doesn't change whether a thing is right or wrong before God. And sometimes, even if we don't know something is a sin, we can still suffer the consequences of our choice. A drug abuser will still suffer the physical consequences of his action, whether or not he sincerely believes drug abuse is morally acceptable.

Question #101

"How can anyone be sinless?" Thang P., 19

A. No one can be sinless on his or her own. Only God can enable a person to remain free of sin. Through no merits of her own, the Blessed Virgin Mary was conceived without original sin by a special grace from God. This is called the Immaculate Conception. She was also preserved from personal sin throughout her life by divine grace. Otherwise, she would have been a sinner like the rest of us. This is why she called God her Savior (Luke 1:47). God saved her from falling into sin, *before* the fact, not after the fact, as with us.

Question #102

"How good do you have to be to go to heaven?" Katie V., 14

A. You can't be good enough on your own to deserve to go to heaven. The Bible and the Catholic Church teach that a person cannot, strictly speaking, *earn* his or her way into heaven. Salvation is the free gift of God through Jesus Christ. But the gift of salvation in Christ must be accepted by us and freely cooperated with. God's grace can transform us so we can live holy lives and receive heaven as our "reward" for our faithfulness to Him.

Salvation means being in proper relationship with God — believing, trusting and loving God, giving ourselves to Him wholly and freely. Baptism puts us in that relationship by communicating to us the forgiveness of Christ and the grace of being a son or daughter of God (John 3:5). However, just because we have been baptized doesn't guarantee we will go to heaven. We can alienate ourselves from God if we willingly disobey God's law and turn our backs on Him through mortal sin. Even so, God is ever-willing to forgive us, especially through the Sacrament of Confession, where Christ cleanses us from our sins committed after Baptism and reconciles us to Himself once again.

Question #103

"Should we do things to be saved or because we are saved? Matthew S., 16

A. First, let's clarify how we are saved. We are saved by grace through faith in Christ (Eph. 2:8), not by our own efforts. In this sense, works *can't* save us. But we must cooperate with grace; faith must be completed by our love and obedience, in order to be living, saving faith (Gal. 5:6, Rom. 1:8, James 2:8-26). Here, works of Christian obedience, motivated by the love of God and neighbor, come into play. Without such works, our faith is dead and cannot save us.

So our cooperation — our "work" in a very limited sense — is necessary for salvation. Yet even our cooperation is a matter of grace. As St. Paul wrote, "Work out your salvation with fear and trembling, for God is at work in you, *both to will and to work for His good pleasure* (my emphasis)" (Phil. 2:12-13). Even when we cooperate with God by doing good, it is God who is inspiring, enabling, and moving us to do so. Our part is not to say "no."

One thing to keep in mind: Being "saved" is more than a "one-time event." It is also a process. There are "three tenses" to salvation. If someone asks, "Are you saved?" you should answer: "I *have been* saved from my sins through Christ's death and resurrection. I *am being* saved as I cooperate with God's grace. And I *will be* saved so long as I do not reject God's love and die in His friendship (i.e., in a state of grace)." Salvation is a past, present and future reality.

Question #104

"Could it be possible for a lot of Mormons, Jews, and Protestants who are not of the true Faith to go to heaven if they have a strong faith?" Ed H., 18

A. Yes. That doesn't mean everything about these faiths is correct. But there are elements of truth there which a person invincibly ignorant of the Catholic Church might follow in good faith. Someone might be saved despite these errors, and because of the power of the truth they do have and the grace of

God with which they freely cooperate. If a person, moved by grace, remains faithful to the truth *as he understands it*, he will be an "unconscious Catholic" and may be saved.

Although someone might be saved under these circumstances, it is better to have the fullness of truth than merely part of the truth mixed with error. It is better to have the fullness of the means of salvation, such as the Sacraments and the teaching authority offered by the Magisterium. This is one reason why we need to carry the Catholic message to the whole world.

Question #105

"If you sin, can you still get into heaven?" Juleane S., 15

A. I hope so, otherwise you and I almost certainly wouldn't make it there. The only way sin can keep us out of heaven is if we die unrepentant of mortal sin. We have already considered why this is so in a previous question, but keep in mind the fact that to sin mortally is to reject God or to choose something incompatible with God's love. If we reject God in this way and die unrepentant, how can we expect to be with Him forever in heaven?

The Bible reminds us if we do sin, God is eager to forgive us. But this requires repentance — being sorry for our sin and intending not to do it again —

and turning back to God. The Sacrament of Confession is the normal way for Catholics to repent and receive forgiveness of sins after Baptism.

Question #106

"Can you enter heaven without being baptized?" Claire H., 14

A. Baptism is the Sacrament by which we are first united to Christ, our sins are washed away, we receive His new life of grace and become sons and daughters of God. It is the entry into the community of God's people, the Church. Consequently, it is necessary for salvation. The person who knowingly and willingly refuses Baptism cannot be saved.

Does that mean all unbaptized persons will be lost? No, for the Church teaches one cannot be saved without Baptism "or the desire of." There is such a thing as "Baptism of desire" by which a person who explicitly or implicitly desires Baptism, but who is incapable of receiving it before death, can be saved. There is also "Baptism of blood," in which those who die for their faith in Christ without having been baptized receive the fruits of the Baptism even without receiving the Sacrament itself.

Question #107

"If you believe in the Lord and love Him, will you have eternal life and get to heaven?" Genny C., 19

A. Yes. Of course our belief must be more than an intellectual nod to certain ideas and our love must be more than warm feelings. Faith that just says "yes" to a bunch of religious ideas cannot save; that "faith" is dead without love (James 2:14-16).

To be saved, we must believe what God says and we must love Him above all things for His own sake and everything else for love of Him. Practically speaking, that means keeping His Commandments. We can't just give God "lip service" — say we'll obey, but then do what we want. "If you love Me," Jesus said, "you will keep My Commandments" (John 14:15). Needless to say, all of this we accomplish by His grace, not our own power.

Question #108

"What does the Catholic Church teach about what our bodies will be like in heaven?" Jesse G., 13

A. We are told in Scripture and in Sacred Tradition that our bodies will be perfected (1 Cor. 15:40-58, Phil 3:21). Theologians have suggested four characteristics that best describe what they will be like: impassable, subtle, agile and clarity.

Our glorified bodies will be *impassable*. They will experience no pain, suffering, weariness, hunger or thirst. Scripture says: "God will wipe away every tear from their eyes, for the former things have passed away" (Rev. 7:21).

We will also have the gift of *subtlety*. We will have a human body with the characteristics of a spirit. Just as Christ could walk through walls after His Resurrection (John 20:19-20), so too should we be able to walk through walls. God will assimilate the characteristics of a spirit to the body without destroying the body's material characteristics.

We will also possess the gift of *agility*, which means we will not be subject to the forces of nature as we were on earth. Our playground will not be limited to the small area we can presently cover with our human powers. Rather, the farthest reaches of the universe will be accessible with the swiftness of a thought. Our body will also respond to the saintly direction of the soul whereas on earth it fought against the good intentions of the will.

Finally, our bodies will have *clarity* in thought and appearance. We will have glorified bodies without the ailments and infirmities of our earthly bodies. Amputations will be mended. Those who are blind will gain sight. Our immortal souls will have a more glorious home in our new bodies.

Question #109

"Why are people afraid of death?" Nathan T., 15

A. There are probably several reasons: (1) People don't have enough faith if they loved God and served

Him on earth that He will embrace them at the time of death. (2) There is a natural fear of the unknown, even if you have faith. (3) Almost every death scene we see in the movies and on television is not a pleasant experience.

If we were to continually see the joyful faces of the canonized saints at the time of their death, our fear of death would greatly decrease, if not disappear.

It would be a good practice to meditate on the joy of seeing God at the time of your death. Scripture says, "As a man thinks, so is he" (Prov. 23:7). If we think and pray about what a joyful experience heaven will be, God may just give us the grace to firmly believe it. You should also develop a devotion to St. Joseph, who is the patron of a happy death.

Question #110

"Does heaven really exist?" Colin S., 14

A. Absolutely. Heaven is the ultimate and final reality for those who die in God's friendship.

Because we get distracted with the good attractions of this world (entertainment, dating, fancy cars, delicious food, etc.), we often forget or even doubt the ultimate good — heaven. As Catholic apologist Scott Hahn has said, "If we fill up on the hors d'oeuvres (snack foods) of life, we will not desire the heavenly banquet."

There are approximately 800 verses that mention heaven in the Bible. The testimony of the Word of God bears witness to its existence.

Question #111
"What is heaven?" Clark K., 14

A. The new *Catechism of the Catholic Church* says that heaven is the kingdom of God which was opened for us by the merits of Christ's death on the cross. Heaven is the place of perfect happiness where the souls of the just see the face of God even before the resurrection of their bodies. Heaven is the eternal community of love with the Father, Son and Holy Spirit, Mary and the angels and all saints (CCC #1023-1029).

Question #112
"What is heaven like?" Robert V., 15

A. Reading about heaven is fascinating. Unfortunately, very few books are out today that address the topic. Perhaps this is why so few seem to be concerned with heaven. Nevertheless, it is worthy of much discussion.

Heaven will be the most profound experience we will ever know. The Bible uses human terms to describe heaven, but these fall far short of the reality. Heaven has been referred to as "eternal life," "holy city," "city of solemnity," "promised land," "everlasting joy" and "perpetual rest." St. Paul tells us that "eye has not seen, and ear has not heard, and it has not entered the human heart, what God has prepared for those who love Him" (1 Cor. 2:9).

Our souls were made for union with God (1 Pet. 4:19, Ps. 31:5). The Beatific Vision (the vision of God) will be our completion. We crave completion. Our souls crave heaven, even though many of us do not know it. Hell is perpetual incompleteness. Hell is the pain of the loss of God. In contrast, heaven is the complete joy found in the possession of God.

Imagine a 10-year-old girl who has been locked in a dark and cold cell all of her life and then is finally set free. She is set free into an endless field of flowers. It's a sea of beauty with no boundaries. She is basking in the warm sun. The little child is allowed to gaze upon and pick the flowers. Each flower is more beautiful than the next. She is truly happy for the first time in her life. She knows she will always remain happy. This example is but a small taste of the endless beauty and joy of heaven.

Did you ever see something so beautiful that you actually lost your breath for a second? In time, however, you were not as moved as when your first saw it. Well, the Beatific Vision will be like that first awe-filled breath. But this breath will never end.

When people see something that is delightful, they occasionally burst into tears with joy. The joy is so intense that tears are the only appropriate response. This too is what the Beatific Vision will be like. Our hearts will be so filled with joy and God's love that they will want to burst.

In heaven, not only will every wish be satisfied, every wish will be *anticipated* by God. We won't even have to wish for anything. It will already be there. In fact, we will be *incapable* of wishing for more than we already have — *because we will have God.*

I can guarantee if you read good Catholics books on heaven and think about it often, you will grow in love and desire for it. When you desire something, you work towards it. There is no goal better to work towards than heaven. And there is no goal more worth reaching.

Question #113

"Can you see things in heaven?" Robert V., 15

A. There seems to be two different types of sight in heaven: the "sight" of the mind and soul and actual physical sight.

We will see God "face-to-face." However, this sight

will be different from the sight used by our material bodies. If I ask you, "Do you see what I mean?"
You are really "seeing" with your mind. This is similar to how we will know God, because God the
Father does not have a body. We will experience
God even more closely than we experience our
own thoughts. We will know God in a much different way than the way we experience things here
on earth with our senses.

We will experience God without anything blocking
the experience. Even thoughts in our mind are
"blocks" to "the real thing." These thoughts are simply mental representations.

The "second sight" is the physical sight we experience on earth. We will literally see Jesus, Mary and
the saints after the general resurrection at the end
of time when our bodies are rejoined to our souls.
However, even after this, our "sight" will be different from our current experience because we will
see God in all creatures we gaze upon.

Based on the doctrine of the Communion of the
Saints, we also believe the saints in heaven do have
some knowledge of those on earth. We will know
and understand the human experience much more
deeply than we do now.

Because God wants all to be happy in heaven,

we will surely see everything necessary for our happiness.

Question #114

"Are there different levels of heaven?" Melissa D., 15

A. The Catholic Church teaches there are different levels of joy in heaven because there are different levels of reward (Matt. 20:21, John 14:1-3). This difference, though, will not cause any jealousy or distance between the saints because all are perfected in charity and perfectly happy in the presence of God.

Here's a frequently used analogy: Imagine your soul is like a glass. In heaven, some people will have a large "glass," others will have a small "glass." Those with a large glass will have more of God's love poured into it (i.e., poured into their soul) because they loved more perfectly on earth. They prepared their soul to receive more of God. The person with a smaller "glass" will still be *completely* filled with God but will hold less of His love. Yet, he or she will want for nothing and will not be jealous of those who received more of God's love.

Question #115

"What is hell?" Philip S., 14

A. Hell is the eternal separation from God and the blessed (CCC #1033). Hell is (or will be) an actual place because the bodies of the resurrected damned will be there. Hell was originally just created for Satan and the other fallen angels who rebelled against God in the beginning of time. However, with the fall of man through original sin we, too, can now go to hell as punishment for unrepented sins against God.

Hell is also referred to as "Gehenna" (Matt. 25:41, Rev. 14:9-11). It has been described as a prison (Job 38:17), a place of torment and misery (Dan. 12:2, Matt. 8:11-12, Luke 13:24-28), a pit (Job 26: 5-6, 2 Pet. 2:4), a place of darkness (Ps. 88:6, Jude 13), an unquenchable fire where the worm does not die (Isaiah 66:24), and a lake of fire (Rev. 19:20). Human images or responses used to describe hell include wailing (crying), gnashing of teeth, pain, stench, unquenchable thirst, binding chains and incredible darkness. There is only hate in hell, especially hate for God.

According to the *Catechism*, hell is "reserved for those who to the end of their lives refuse to believe and be converted" (CCC #1034). Because God is just, only those who are truly worthy of hell will go there. It is for those who die in a state of mortal sin and who intentionally do not repent before death. References in the Bible to hell as a punishment for sin include Isaiah 3:11, Rom. 2:6, 1 Cor. 6:9-10 and more.

Few doctrines in Scripture are more frequently affirmed than hell. There are many references to hell in Scripture, including a dozen from Jesus Himself. The existence of hell is a dogma of the faith that Catholics are required to believe.

Question #116

"What kind of pain or punishment do you endure in hell?" Clare H., 14

A. Hell is the exclusion of being in our majestic God's presence (Matt. 5:20, 7:21-23, Luke 12:24-28, 1 Cor. 6:9-11, Gal. 5:21, 2 Thess. 1:9). This is the primary pain of hell.

Human beings were made for union with God and are intended to be with Him for all eternity. Some theologians speculate a person in hell will be forced to contemplate his intended destiny with God and how his selfishness kept him from this. He will see the emptiness of his excessive self-love and will have a vivid knowledge of his offenses. He will also see the many gifts God offered and how he rejected them.

Is the "fire" of hell literal or merely symbolic of severe punishment? Theologians differ about that. Certainly, hellfire is different in many respects from the ordinary fire we know. Scripture speaks of hell as the "outer darkness," which is hard to understand if hellfire is like the fire we know. Also, the fire of hell is perpetual and capable of punishing spiritual beings — again, something very different from conventional fire.

We know from Scripture that God is love (1 John 4:8). Because those in hell are cut off from the source of love (God), they will hate God. The souls in hell will know the goodness of God and will hate it.

Again, the most painful part of hell is the incompleteness we will always feel because we will not have union with God. It will be a perpetual frustration and torment that will never end.

Question #117

"How could there be a place like hell if Jesus loves people unconditionally?" Jennifer N., 17

A. Because Jesus loves people so much He gives them the tremendous gift of freedom. That means if they chose to reject Him, He will not force Himself upon them. Those who finally reject Him get what they want — to be left alone by God. That is the horrendous reality we call hell.

Here are seven reasons why a place like hell is reasonable to believe in and, despite it's horrendousness, is still compatible with God's love:

1) What else can God do with the man? If a man dies loving himself more than God, what can God do with him? He has to let him go to the place of his own making. He can't take him to heaven and force him to love Him, for that would mean an inconceivably close union with God, Whom the man hates. Loving God (and being close to Him) would be a ceaseless torment to the man, who really loves himself most of all. It is impossible for man to reject God and possess Him at the same time.

2) Jesus (and the Father) wouldn't lie. God the Father and the Son (Jesus) reveal many times in Scripture that hell is real. How then could God say, "I was only kidding." God doesn't kid about something as serious as hell. It must be true.

3) God is justice and love together. God is not 51 percent love and 49 percent justice or vice versa. God is 100 percent justice and 100 percent love at the same time. By His very nature (perfection), God is incapable of an injustice. Therefore, eternal punishment must somehow be just.

Our free will is a gift that is in accord with our dignity as human beings. It would be an injustice for God to force us to love Him because this would go against our nature as humans. It would not offer the challenge or choice that our intellects and free will deserve. It would be an injustice for Him *not* to allow us to use our free will to choose or reject Him. Therefore, hell can actually be an argument *for* the justice of God.

4) Because the offense is so serious, the punishment must be just. If a person assaults another person, he may go to prison for a year. If he assaults the mayor, he will go to prison for a longer time. If he assaults the president of the United States, he'll go for an even longer time. And, if he assaults the eternal God, by rejecting Him and His laws, it's not unreasonable to think he should go to "prison" for all eternity. Why? The penalty is measured by the gravity of the offense and the importance of the person we assault. Rejecting an infinite God (and not repenting) merits an infinite punishment.

5) God does not condemn men to hell. We condemn ourselves. God simply allows it because He knows that because the man rejected Him, it is just. God gives us every possible aid to avoid hell. He gave His only Son. He gave us the Church and the pope to teach us. He gave us the Bible as written documentation of His truth. He gave us the Eucharist to nourish us spiritually. He gave us Confession to heal us spiritually. He even gave us the Anointing of the Sick for those who are close to death. He gave us miracles to help us believe. *Yet, people still reject Him.* They couldn't care less about Him or His laws. What is God to do with them without offending their human dignity and free will?

6) Because man would live a more sinful life if there weren't the threat of hell. The possibility of spend-

ing eternity in hell is a great deterrent for bad behavior. Hell is an "emergency brake" against a life of
sin. Time has proven that, because of our sinful nature and love of self, too many men choose to live
for themselves instead of God. *And this is in a world
that mostly believes that hell exists.* Can you imagine
what life would be like if Christianity taught that
there was a second chance after this life? Many would
act much differently. Many would say, "I'm going to
live it up here on earth because I plan to repent in
the next life." We would have chaos. We would have
much more abortion, homicide, premarital sex, etc.

*7) If punishment on earth is OK, why not in the af-
terlife?* For those of you who reject the idea of eternal punishment, why do you not reject temporal
(earthly) punishment? Why have prisons? Why have
traffic tickets for speeding violations? Why have penalties for crimes here on earth if you're not prepared
to have penalties for crimes committed against the
One who made the earth? Penalties for crimes are
necessary in order to maintain earthly justice and
order. Likewise, penalties for crimes against God are
necessary in order to maintain justice and order in
the spiritual realm.

It's important to remember you are in *no danger of
hell* if you simply stay faithful to God and His laws.
God will help us. And, if you fall into sin, get back
up and be reconciled through the confessional.

God does not take pleasure in allowing people to go to hell. Nor should we. This would be a warped view of justice. We should want all to be saved. We should always pray the Our Lady of Fatima prayer at the end of each decade of the rosary which says in part, "Lead all souls to heaven, especially those in most need of Thy mercy."

Question #118

"What is purgatory?" Megann R., 15

A. Purgatory is the state of purification that some souls must undergo before receiving the Beatific Vision, the vision of God. Purgatory is an infallible dogma of the Faith.

Purgatory is for people who are destined for heaven, but who have venial sins on their souls or the effects of *forgiven* mortal sins, which must be cleansed (Matt. 5:26). Because "nothing unclean shall enter" into heaven (Rev. 21:27), God has established a place of final purification, purgatory.

Purgatory is not a "second chance." If one dies in mortal sin, he goes directly to hell. If one dies in a state of grace and has completely formed his will and love of God to a state of perfection, he will go straight to heaven.

At our personal judgments after death (Heb. 9:27, 2 Cor. 5:8), we will know our past life as never before.

If we get saved but are still attached to the vestiges (remnants) of sin, we will not only see the justice and logic of purgatory, but will actually *want* to go there. As C.S. Lewis once wrote, "Our souls demand purgatory, don't they?" No questions will arise; no justification will be offered. We will adore and humble ourselves before Jesus when we first meet Him, but then want to leave His presence because it would be an insult to Him for us to stay.

When we sin, we love ourselves more than God and His laws. This is disordered love. This sin is like the impurities found in newly mined gold. To make the gold perfect, we need to put it through fire. The fire "sweats out" the impurities. This is analogous to the purification process in purgatory (1 Cor. 3:12-13).

There's a common objection directed at the Church by Protestants that the doctrine of purgatory "takes away from the work of Jesus on the cross at Calvary" and is therefore unbiblical. This is not true. Purgatory is an *application of* the cross. Jesus' death is so powerful that it can actually purify us in the afterlife. The souls in purgatory are purged of their sin by their sharing in the sufferings of Christ.

Question #119

"What kind of pain or punishment do you endure in purgatory?" Clare H., 14

A. There are two primary feelings going on at the

same time in purgatory: sadness and joy. We have sadness because we are not with God and yet are yearning for Him. We have joy because we know we are saved and will soon be with Him. Let me speak about both aspects in greater detail.

The pains in purgatory have often been referred to in terms of "fire." This has developed because of certain biblical texts, including 1 Corinthians 3:15, and also because of purgatory's alleged association with hell. Other have said the fires are merely a metaphor for the intense pain we will experience in our yearning for God. The Church has not defined whether fire is a part of purgatory.

You've heard the phrase "burning love." This is the feeling in purgatory. When you love someone, you want to be with them. If you can't be with them, there's pain. The greater the unfulfilled desire, the greater the pain. God is the ultimate good. Once we are saved, every fiber of our being will long for the vision of the Father. The degree of pain in purgatory is directly in proportion to our realization of the greatness of God and our choice in rejecting His graces during our earthly life.

Regarding the joys of purgatory, consider this story: Imagine you've grown to love someone from a foreign country very deeply after 50 years of writing letters to each other. You've never met the person, but have come to know him through the letters. Your love grew deeper each week because of the intimacy you've both experienced from the letters. You then receive a train ticket to visit him. As the train you're on nears the station, your excitement builds. You are about to meet your love after 50 years of friendship! You look out the train window and see someone in the distance. It's him! You are incredibly excited about this face-to-face visit.

This is similar to the joy of purgatory. Your love is being perfected in purgatory and your burning desire to see God is increasing by the second. The pain of this love is greater than any pain ever experienced because you are not with God, but the joy in knowing you will soon be with Him for all eternity makes the suffering worth it.

Question #120

"How can I persuade my Protestant friends that purgatory exists?" Jesse G., 13

A. First find out what they believe purgatory is and why they object to it. Chances are they misunderstand the doctrine.

Then explain how both you and your friend agree that Jesus wants us to be holy. Remind your friends that Jesus said, "Be perfect as your Father in heaven is perfect" (Matt. 5:48). Point out that Hebrews 12:14 instructs us to "strive for that holiness without which no one will see the Lord" and Revelation 21:27 declares that "nothing unclean shall enter heaven." Explain that while Jesus took away our sins on the cross, we must still be sanctified (made holy) by the Holy Spirit. If we are not perfectly sanctified in this life, then we must be in the next, in order to enter heaven.

The Old and New Testaments support belief in purgatory. Although the *word* "purgatory" is not mentioned by name (nor are the words "trinity" and "incarnation"), the *truth* is there. In the second book of Maccabees, we read: "It is a holy and wholesome thought to pray for the dead that they might be loosed from their sins" (2 Macc. 12:46). The early Protestants didn't include 2 Maccabees in their version of the Bible because they couldn't reconcile what it taught with their rejection of purgatory. In doing so, they rejected a millennia of Tradition in denying this truth.

In the New Testament we read that some will be saved, "but only as through fire" (1 Cor. 3:15). We also read, "The judge will hand you over to the guard, and you will be thrown into prison. Amen, I say to you, you will not be released until you have paid the last penny. (Matt. 5:25-26)."

Question #121

"Can we actually help those in purgatory get out by our prayers?" Ed H., 18

A. Yes. The members of the body of Christ are connected to each other. The Church refers to three types of Christians: the Church Militant (those on earth), the Church Triumphant (those in heaven) and the Church Suffering (those in purgatory). We are all part of the same mystical body of Christ, whether in heaven, on earth or in purgatory.

The Bible exhorts us to pray for one another (1 Tim. 2:1-4, 2 Macc. 12:46). This prayer includes *all* members of the body, especially those in need. Those in purgatory are in need because they can't help themselves.

Our prayers, especially the Mass, are said to relieve the suffering of the holy souls in purgatory. These souls are eternally grateful for our prayers and will remember us when they get to heaven. If we go to purgatory, they will surely pray for us. Praying for the dead is an obligation for Catholics, so keep up this good and holy practice.

Question #122

"What are the 'end times?'" Christopher H., 19

A. The "end times" are often considered the final period of human history, prior to the Second Coming of Christ.

The Bible also speaks of the "last days." Are we living in the "last days?" Yes, and we have been for nearly two thousand years (Acts. 2:17). The "last days" began with the Death, Resurrection and Ascension of Christ and the outpouring of the Spirit on Pentecost (CCC #670).

Scripture and even some approved apparitions also see the end times as a period of tribulation, chastisement, purification and eventual peace right before Jesus' actual return.

Question #123

"When do you think the world will end?" Jessica C., 13

A. Thank goodness I don't know the date because that would cause tremendous emotional stress to me and to those whom I told. Scripture says that no one except the Father knows the time when the end will come (Matt. 24:36).

The only thing we do know for sure is that it will happen at the appropriate time. It will happen when some goal of all mankind has been achieved, according to Catholic apologist Frank Sheed in his book *Theology for Beginners*. Sheed proposes it would be silly to think that God will suddenly lose patience with wayward mankind. God knew when He created the world when it would end.

The end will come when all who are to be incorporated into the Church are incorporated into it. There will be no need for more people. Humanity would have fulfilled its purpose, which is the delivering of the Good News to all. (Matt. 28:19)

Question #124

"Will there be signs to tell us the world is going to end?" Erinn T., 16

A. Scripture says that there will be some signs we can look for including a great apostasy (falling away) from the Catholic Church and the arrival of the anti-Christ, who will be a man, not a demon (Dan. 11).

This anti-Christ will be someone who is aided by Satan. As Christ had the prophet John the Baptist as his herald, the anti-Christ will have the "false prophet" as his herald. Scripture also mentions a mass conversion of the Jewish people after they recognize Jesus as the Messiah for Whom they awaited (Rom. 11:26).

Question #125

"What Catholic miracles have occurred?" Colin S., 14

A. They are too numerous to count. To begin, all miracles of Jesus are considered Catholic miracles because He is the founder of our Faith. These miracles included the multiplication of the loaves, the turning of water into wine at the wedding feast at Cana, the raising of Lazarus from the dead, and Jesus' own Resurrection, among many others.

There have also been many miracles after Jesus ascended into heaven. We have Eucharistic miracles where, after the consecration, the Body of Jesus (formerly the bread) and the Blood of Jesus (formerly the wine) have actually turned to visible flesh and blood. These can be seen today.

We also have miracles where the bodies of dead saints have not corrupted hundreds of years after their deaths. There is also the miracle of the tilma (cloak) that Blessed Juan Diego was wearing when he saw the apparition of Our Lady of Guadalupe, Mexico. The tilma has a miraculous image of Our Lady on it. The tilma itself should have withered away since it is over 450 years old, but it has not. Science is unable to explain any of these miracles.

You may want to contact a local Catholic bookstore for a good book on the subject.

Question #126

"Can you describe the role Mary plays in Catholicism? I know she was chosen to be the Mother of God, but can you go into more detail?" Vanessa C., 16

A. Mary said "yes" to God when the angel Gabriel

announced to her the divine plan that she would be the Mother of the Savior. She became the human instrument God chose to bring about salvation. It was from her that Christ took His human nature. She is our human link to Him.

Adam and Eve's "no" to God was enough to cast all mankind into darkness and death, until the Savior would come. This is why the Church acknowledges that Mary's "yes" cooperated in some way with the salvation of mankind.

Mary must be special. Out of all the billions of people in history, she was chosen to be the one who would bear God in her womb. She would be the one to nurse, play with and teach the infant Jesus, who is God. This is a *big* task.

Mary is also an intercessor for us. The first record of her intercession was at the wedding feast of Cana where she asked her Son to assist when the wine ran out (John 2:3-11). Jesus responded by performing His first recorded miracle. Since that day, Mary has interceded continually for us. She does this each time we invoke her in prayer.

Question #127

"How can a Catholic explain to non-Catholics how wonderful and good the Blessed

Virgin Mary is and how we don't worship her but rather ask her to pray to God for us?" Kelly T., 15

A. Jesus was a good Jewish boy who kept the Commandments perfectly. The Fourth Commandment requires us to "Honor thy father and mother." The Hebrew word for "honor" also means to "glorify." So, Jesus "glorified" His mother. Our goal as Christians is to imitate Jesus. We, too, should "glorify" His mother. She is the mother of our Lord.

The real question you should ask your non-Catholic friends is, "Why are you *not* giving Mary high recognition? She played a very important role in our salvation by allowing the Father to give us the Son through her." If we can honor Thomas Jefferson or a modern sports hero, why can't we honor a great saint like Mary.

Regarding the "worship" of Mary, the Catholic Church would seriously condemn the worship of Mary, who is a creature. Worship, or *"latria"* in Latin, is reserved for God alone.

However, the Church encourages us to give her the special recognition she deserves. We are allowed to give the saints *"dulia,"* which in Latin means "praise." And, we are allowed to give Mary *"hyper-dulia,"* which in Latin means "extra praise." Catholic teaching on Mary expresses the biblical idea that Mary is "blessed among women" (Lk. 1:42) and that "all generations" shall call her blessed (Lk. 1:48).

Question #128

"What is the pope's role?" Michael W., 14

A. As the successor to St. Peter, the pope's role is to be an earthly father to the people of God. (The word "pope" means "father.") He is also the shepherd appointed by the greatest Shepherd of them all — Jesus (John 21:15-17). As Peter led the apostolic college, so his successor, the pope, leads the episcopal college of bishops. In this capacity, he confirms his brother bishops and priests in the Faith (Lk. 22:32), and works with them to spread the Gospel and to pastor the flock of God.

The pope protects the deposit of Faith given to the Church 2,000 years ago by Jesus. He does not make new doctrine, nor can he change a doctrine to mean something different than it had meant in the past. His role is to pass on the Faith to the Church.

Question #129

"How does the pope get elected by the Church?" Guy C., 14

A. Upon the death of the pope and after a traditional nine-day period of mourning has passed, the college of cardinals in an electoral session (or conclave) chooses the one whom they believe the Holy Spirit has guided them to choose. The new pope must be named on at least two-thirds of the ballots plus one.

Shortly after the selection is made, the pope is then asked by the head of the college if he accepts the nomination. If he says yes, he is then asked, "What will you be called?" After this, the ballots where the names were written are burned and this gives us the "white smoke," which is the signal to the world that a new pope has been chosen. An announcement is then made in Latin: "I bring you a message of great joy. We have a pope, (his birth name), who has chosen the name (his new name)."

Question #130

"How can the pope be totally infallible? If he is, why does he not win the lottery?" Paul K., 13

A. The pope isn't "totally infallible." His infallibility extends only to matters of faith and morals, and it can operate only when he is defining something pertaining to faith or morals for the whole Church.

Infallibility is a special gift given by God to the Church to protect it from teaching as true what is, in fact, false. It is not new revelation, but a special protection to ensure the Faith will not be distorted by error.

The pope has no "hotline" to God. He must get his doctrine the same way we do — he must pray and study. Infallibility says only after he has done his study and when he defines something as part of the Catholic Faith, the Holy Spirit protects what he teaches from being wrong. It refers to his function as official teacher, not as a private person, nor even as a private theologian.

Not only the pope, but all the bishops of the Church in union with the pope are protected from teaching error, when they meet to define a matter of faith or morals or when, scattered throughout the world, they agree on how a matter of faith or morals is to be definitively held.

Because it applies only to matters of faith or morals, the gift of infallibility does not mean the pope can't be wrong about the winning lottery numbers. Nor is he guaranteed to correctly predict the winner of the Super Bowl.

Also, infallibility is not inspiration. This means the pope isn't automatically given the proper words with which to teach. Infallibility is a *negative protection*. The Holy Spirit will never allow the Pope to teach as truth *something which is actually false*.

Sometimes infallibility is also confused with "impeccability," which is the idea that the pope is sinless or cannot sin. That's not what infallibility means. A pope could live a sinful life, as a few popes have, yet his teaching would still be protected by the Holy Spirit. This is the point of infallibility — to protect the Church's teaching from error. A pope may end up in hell for a sinful life, but his teaching would still have been protected by the Holy Spirit.

Here are the conditions necessary for infallible teaching by the pope:

1) The pope must make it clear he is exercising his supreme *ex cathedra* ("from the chair," which refers to his office as teacher) authority;

2) He is defining a matter pertaining to faith or morals;

3) The pope must use terms which make it clear he is rendering an infallible judgement;

4) He must address the whole Church, not just a part of it;

5) He must make it clear that his teaching binds the consciences of the faithful.

Question #131

"Why can't we eat meat on Fridays in Lent?"
Rachel P., 13

A. The Church asks us to abstain from meat as a

means of sacrifice. The Church only asks us to do what is ultimately good for us. It is not a mean-spirited "killjoy" whose purpose is to make life tough for us. The Church is truly working in our best interest.

Abstaining from meat is a part of a whole penitential approach to Friday that should be maintained throughout the year, and especially in Lent. As a young person, you did not grow up in an environment when all Fridays throughout the year were days of abstinence from meat. Yet, even today, we are obliged to do some form of penance.

We do penance for several reasons: (1) as a way to expiate or atone for our sins of the past, (2) to learn to master our instincts (which will help us fight sin), (3) to help us prepare for the spiritual feast of the Resurrection of Jesus on Easter, (4) as a sign of our conversion, (5) and as a way to purify our soul (CCC #2043).

Mastering the little challenges in life prepares us for the big challenges. A person who can't even control little challenges like abstaining from meat one day a week is more likely to fall prey to more difficult challenges.

The rules for days of fasting are that we can eat one full meal and two small meals which together add up to no more than one meal. Abstinence days have the same requirements as the fast days and also involve the avoidance of meat for that day only.

Question #132

"Why do we go to church on Sunday vs. another day?" Erik L., 14

A. Saturday was the Sabbath for the Jews, but the early Catholics changed the practice to Sunday to commemorate Jesus' rising from the dead on Sunday.

For the first Jewish Christians, both Saturday (the original Sabbath) and Sunday were regarded as festival days. As the number of Jewish converts to Christianity decreased, the observance of Saturday as a holy day diminished.

For the gentile (non-Jewish) Christians, Saturday never had any importance. They only observed Sunday as the holy day.

There have been attempts by modern Protestant sects to re-establish Saturday as the day of worship. The most notable sect is the Seventh-Day Adventists. This belief has virtually no historical basis and is contrary to the spirit of the early Church and will of God.

Question #133

"Where does holy water come from and what is its purpose?" Megann R., 15

A. Holy water is actually just ordinary water that has been blessed and to which some salt has been added. The salt signifies our future preservation from corruption. Its purpose is to remind us of our Baptism and to signify we are not worthy to enter into the presence of Christ without first being purified. Holy water also washes away venial sin.

Question #134

"How does one become a priest?" Charles C., 13

A. By first contacting the local diocese or a religious order. The process includes some psychological evaluation to determine whether you are a good prospect for the trials and demands of ministry. This evaluation may also focus on your views, beliefs and ability to interact socially and pastorally, which is almost always needed in such an important form of work. Another important thing will be an assessment of your reasons for wanting to become a priest.

After one is accepted, the applicant will receive spiritual, academic, psychological and social guidance to prepare him for ministry. This can be a rewarding (but lengthy) training process and will include a firm grounding in the doctrines of the Church. Some dioceses even require special language training. All this is to prepare the future priest for ordination and the challenges ahead in his life of service to the Lord.

Naturally, each diocese has different needs so this makes indentifying the exact "characteristics" of the desired type of priest very difficult to pinpoint. Canon Law does require that a priest be at least 25 years old. (Can. 1031)

Question #135

"Why aren't Catholic priests allowed to marry?" Amy F., 14

A. Although the early Church allowed married clergy, the Church later came to see celibacy as a better example of the norm and model of Jesus' priesthood.

In referring to celibacy, St. Paul says: "Indeed, I wish everyone to be as I am, but each has a particular gift from God...Now to the unmarried and to widows I say: it is a good thing for them remain as they are, as I do" (1 Cor. 7:7-8). He goes on to say: "An unmarried man is anxious about the things of the Lord, how he may please the Lord. But the married man is anxious about the things of the world, how he may please his wife, and he is divided" (1 Cor. 7:32-34).

Jesus said: "Everyone who has given up house or brothers or sisters or father or mother or children or lands for the sake of My name will receive a hundred times more, and will inherit eternal life" (Matt. 19:29).

Celibacy is a discipline, not a dogma. This means that the Church could change the rule. However, this is unlikely because of the many positive and practical benefits of celibacy. Here are 10 reasons why a celibate clergy makes good sense:

1) It leaves the priest free to more fully commit his life to the service of the Lord and the laity.

2) The Church has found it is better to keep priests moving from parish to parish every few years perhaps for a few reasons, including the desire to prevent a cult of personality from building around a particular priest. This situation can put too much focus on the man vs. his message. So, the church prudently moves priests around. Can you imagine how much stress it would cause a priest to have to move a wife and family each time? Having a celibate priesthood enables the bishop, to whom the priest dedicates his life at ordination, the full flexibility he needs to move priests around.

3) To be able to lay their life down for their flock. Because a celibate priest does not have the obligation of a wife and children, he can give himself more easily, including his own life, if necessary. For example, Blessed Damien de Veuster of Belgium was

able to work with lepers on the island of Molokai, Hawaii, because of the freedom he had in being a celibate minister. This work eventually lead to his contracting and dying from leprosy.

4) It is a sign of contradiction and challenge to a society that is flooded with sexual messages. Celibacy surely gains the Catholic clergy a hidden respect from many people.

5) It gives the priest greater credibility when he asks the laity to make sacrifices because the laity knows that celibacy involves sacrifice.

6) It helps the priest master his passions, which will help as he teaches and ministers to the laity. It also gives him more time for prayer, which is the lifeblood of any ministry.

7) It enables a priest to be more objective when counseling married couples. He is less likely to project his own marriage successes or problems onto the couple.

8) It enables the priest to be a "spiritual father" to many more people than a married man.

9) It allows the Church to put the hundreds of millions of dollars it saves in priestly salaries to the evangelization and charitable assistance of a needy

world. Although priests do receive salaries, they are much less than they would have to be if they had families to support.

10) It's a foreshadowing that there will be no marriage in heaven.

No one is required to live a permanently celibate life. The Church says that people are free to marry. In fact, the Church glorifies the married state. Only if one wants to become a priest, brother or religious sister do they have to live a celibate life. The religious life, and the requirements that come with it, do not have to be chosen by anyone. However, when it is chosen, it needs to be followed in the manner our Lord and His Church requires.

Sure, celibacy can be difficult, especially in this sexually permissive age. But if a priest has good seminary formation that strongly supports celibacy and if he stays close to our Lord in prayer, he will be able to turn this sacrifice into a wonderful aid to his work.

Question #136

"Can a man cease to be a priest if he gets married?" Christopher R., 15

A. Strictly speaking, once a man is validly ordained, he remains a priest forever (Ps. 110:4, Heb. 5:6). He may, however, be relieved of the obligations of priestly ministry. This can happen by laicization, whereby a priest gets special permission to stop ministering as a priest. If he desires marriage, he must also get dispensed from his sacred promise of celibacy.

Once laicized, the man would still have priestly powers to forgive sins and consecrate the Eucharist, but he would be forbidden to do so, except in emergency circumstances.

Question #137

"Don't you think a lot more men would become priests if they were allowed to get married?" Brian K., 13

A. A married priesthood *might* increase the numbers in the short-run, but the real issue is, "Does God really want a married priesthood?" I have already explained the advantages of a celibate priesthood. And furthermore, it is not at all clear that allowing a married priesthood would necessarily substantially increase the number of priests.

Just because a man, married or unmarried, thinks he's called to priestly ministry doesn't mean he is — or that he has the qualifications to serve effectively as a priest. That has to be discerned.

The real problem with priestly vocations today is that many men have lost the spiritual awareness necessary to hear and answer God's call to priestly ministry. They are unwilling to make the personal sacrifices necessary to serve as priests. Ordaining married men would only mean that one less sacrifice would be required of men already disinclined to live a completely sacrificial life, which is the essence of priestly ministry. That doesn't seem to be a recipe for good priests.

Question #138

"Why aren't women allowed to be priests?" Megan M., 14

A. The Church's teaching about the male-only priesthood is difficult for some people today to accept. They overlook the fact there are two crucial truths about gender, equality and difference, not just one — equality.

Jesus made the priesthood a male thing — like fatherhood. It has nothing to do with men being superior to women — they aren't. Men and women are equal in their human dignity; they are equally made "in the image of God." But such equality does not mean "sameness" in all respects, nor does it mean men and women must be entirely interchangeable or that they cannot have different roles in a community.

Furthermore, because some women have been unjustly discriminated against in society and by some Church members, some assume that allowing only men to be priests must be an injustice. But it isn't.

Jesus is the One Who established the priesthood, and He's the One who called only men to be priests. People sometimes say He did this because of the prevailing customs of His time. This is not a strong argument. Jesus freely broke with those customs in other instances, especially regarding women — for example by allowing women to be among His close followers, by addressing them in public and by up-holding their rights in marriage on the same terms as men. That He didn't call any women to be priests is a clear indication He intended priestly ministry to be exclusively male.

Further evidence of this is His mother, the Blessed Virgin. As Pope John Paul II has said, "the fact that the Blessed Virgin Mary, the Mother of God and Mother of the Church, received neither the mission proper to the Apostles nor the ministerial priesthood clearly shows that the non-admission of women to priestly ordination cannot mean that women are of less dignity, nor can it be construed as discrimination against them" (*Ordinatio Sacredotalis*, no. 3). "Rather," he writes, "it is to be seen as the faithful observance of a plan to be ascribed to the Wisdom of the Lord of the Universe."

The Church doesn't have the authority to change what Christ has established. Even if the pope wanted to, he couldn't allow women priests because the Church isn't the pope's Church, it is Christ's Church.

Perhaps it might help to consider why the priesthood is an exclusively masculine thing. The Church itself has always been considered in "feminine" terms. We speak of the Church as the Bride of Christ. Even the term "Body of Christ" is linked to the femininity of the Church by St. Paul in Ephesians, chapter 5. There the Church is the "Body of Christ" because she is "one flesh" or "one body" with Christ, as the wife is one flesh or one body with her husband.

Why is the Church feminine? One reason is because she receives grace from outside herself and nourishes the new life of believers within herself as a mother nourishes her unborn children from within. This is why we sometimes speak of the Church as "Holy Mother Church."

What has this to do with male priests? The priest is a sacramental sign of Christ as Bridegroom of the Church — an inherently male identity. It is no accident that the Second Person of the Trinity became a male human being. His identity in relation to God's people is masculine and their relation as a people is feminine.

The male priest stands in the person of Christ (*in*

persona Christi, in Latin). He is a sacramental sign of Christ the Bridegroom (Matt. 9:15; 25:1-12; John 3:27-30; Eph. 5) before the Church, His bride. It wouldn't make sense for a woman to try to fulfill this role, anymore than it would for a man to try to be a "mother." There is no inequality here, only the God-given difference between men and women.

Question #139
"Why aren't women more respected in the Church when the greatest of all women gave birth to Jesus?" Clark K., 14

A. Women are held in very high esteem in the Church. In fact, 85 percent of all Church positions are held by women, according to *Catholic Update*, a national newsletter. Pope John Paul II said in his letter *Women: Teachers of Peace*: "When women are able fully to share their gifts with the whole community, the very way in which society understands and organizes itself is improved...The growing presence of women in social, economic and political life...is thus a very positive development...This acknowledgment of their public roles however should not detract from their role within the family...Here their contribution to the welfare and progress of society, even if its importance is not sufficiently appreciated, is truly incalculable."

Countless holy women have established religious orders; built monasteries, hospitals and orphanages; and they have taught tens of millions of our children. In fact, someone once told me that Catholic nuns were running schools *before women in the secular world were allowed to even attend them.*

Although some members of the Church have made mistakes regarding the role of women in the past, the Church has been far ahead of society in acknowledging their true importance and allowing them to share their gifts with the Church.

Question #140

"Is feminism compatible with Catholicism?" Maria O., 18

A. It depends on what you mean by feminism. If you mean women should have the same basic human rights as men, then certainly Catholic teaching agrees. If by feminism you mean there should be no social distinctions between men and women or for true equality to exist between genders in the Church women must be ordained to the priesthood, then the answer is "no."

The latter view is sometimes called "secular" or "radical feminism." Some views commonly held by secular or radical feminists are actually contrary to true feminine dignity. For example, a woman's ability to conceive and bear children is a wonderful gift from

God. Yet many radical feminists view child-bearing as little better than a curse. They support things which actually degrade women, such as contraception and abortion.

Question #141

"Are angels male, female, both or neither?" Christina C., 18

A. We have no evidence from revelation that angels are male or female. Being pure spirits, they cannot possess the bodily traits of gender. Even so, angels are sometimes depicted in male or female forms. This is probably so we can better relate to them on a human level. When on the rare occasion an angel appears to human beings, it comes in the form of a male or female human being, even though it is a pure spirit without a body.

Question #142

"Why can't humans become angels, or can we?" Shannon L., 17

A. Contrary to popular myth, we *don't* become angels when we die. Human beings and angels are completely different species of beings. Comparing them is like comparing a human to a cat or a dog, only the difference is much greater.

Angels are pure spirits. Human beings, on the other hand, are beings of body and spirit. Although our bodies and spirits separate at death, this is an un-natural condition for humans. We will be complete persons again only in the Resurrection of the Body; angels, however, are completely themselves right now as pure spirits without bodies.

Question #143

"Can we lose our guardian angels?" Maria O., 18

A. No. Angels are a wonderful gift from God desig-nated to protect and pray for us. They are more faithful and loving than any human being could con-ceive of being because they are pure spirits commit-ted to the Will of God. The Will of God is for all to be saved and come to the knowledge of the truth (1 Tim. 2:4). Therefore, God would never withdraw their support. We can, however, resist their efforts and avoid God's grace. But they will continually be there, in good times and bad.

Question #144

"Is it true that Satan was originally from heaven and fell from grace? If so, how and why did this occur?" Melissa C., 16

A. Catholic teaching states at the beginning of time, God created Satan as a good angel. Satan is said to have been the most glorious of created beings, thus his name Lucifer or "light bearer." Then Satan and his angels became evil by their own doing. They chose not to serve God. They desired to exalt themselves above their created condition and make themselves independent of God and, thus, divine.

This act was a final one against God. The *Catechism* says: "There is no repentance for the angels after their fall, just as there is no repentance for men after death." (CCC #393).

Scripture comments clearly on the subject. Jesus said, "Out of my sight, you condemned, into that everlasting fire prepared for the devil and his angels" (Matt. 25:41). God did not spare the angels when they sinned, but condemned them to the chains of Tartarus (a name which meant "infernal region" in Greek mythology).

The book of Revelation tells of the battle between St. Michael the Archangel and Satan. Satan and his angels were defeated and cast out of heaven (Rev. 12:3-9).

Question #145

"What does the devil look like?" Jimmy C., 14

A. As a spirit, Satan has no physical appearance. Nevertheless, he is often depicted as a malevolent beast. And like other angels, he can assume an earthly appearance.

In Genesis, Satan is described as a beguiling serpent (Gen. 3:1); in the book of Revelation, a dragon (Rev. 12:3). In art he is often depicted as a beast with horns or a dark, bat-like figure, sometimes with a goat's head. Saints such as John Vianney and Stanislaus have seen him in the form of a dog.

But the most dangerous form the devil assumes is as an angel of light (2 Cor. 11:14). In this way, he appears to be good but in fact remains evil.

Images of the devil as imps with pitchforks and tails can also be dangerous if they cause us not to take the devil seriously. That, of course, is part of Satan's plan. He is never so successful as when we make light of, or deny, his existence. As C.S. Lewis noted, the devil's greatest success is to get us to deny that he exists. Why? Because then we shall not be on guard against him.

Question #146

"Is the Catholic religion the only religion that has saints?" David A., 15

A. All who have made it to heaven are saints. They also happen to be Catholic saints, even if they were originally from another religion, because they now understand and accept the truth, which is Catholicism.

The Eastern Orthodox faith (which broke off from the Catholic Church in the year 1054) also recognizes saints. Protestant faiths and many non-Christians religions have "holy men and women" whom they recognize and honor, but these people are not formally recognized as canonized saints by the Church, even though they may be in heaven.

Question #147

"What is a good response to why Catholics wear scapulars?" Christina C., 18

A. The scapular is a small piece of cloth that is a part of the Carmelite Order, a religious community. Those who wear the scapular are, to a certain degree, affiliated with that order and share in their prayers and good works. As a result of this affiliation and a sharing in the order's special devotion to the Mother of Christ, those who wear the scapular in a spirit of true devotion and love have a special claim to Mary's intercession and protection.

On the surface, some people may think scapulars are superstitious "good luck charms" that guarantee our entrance into heaven. They do not. Only living in a state of grace will guarantee us eternal salvation. However, scapulars are a special gift from God by which we attain protective graces.

The Blessed Virgin Mary appeared to St. Simon Stock in the year 1251. She promised that all who wear the brown scapular "shall not suffer eternal fire; and, if wearing it when they die, they shall be saved." This assumes, of course, that one does not deliberately lead a sinful life and make a mockery of God's law.

Question #148

"Why do altars contain relics within them?"
Ed H., 18

A. The Eucharist is the sacrificial offering of Christ to the Father for us. By means of the Holy Spirit, martyrs united themselves and their sacrifices with the sacrifice of Christ on Calvary. Hence it was fitting that the Eucharist be celebrated over their burial sites. Also, the Eucharist is the presence of the Risen Christ. Offering the Mass at Christian burial sites pointed to the Christian expectation of the resurrection of the body.

As time passed, there were more churches than holy sites. So the Church decided to bring the relic to the church instead of the church to the site of the relic. It was decided to place small pieces of relics in the actual altars in churches.

Chapter 10
Catholic Morality

Question #149

"Are Catholics allowed to have an abortion for any reason?" Katie V., 14

A. Since abortion is the direct taking of an innocent human life, one may not deliberately have an abortion or assist another in doing so for any reason. I realize there are difficult situations, such as when a pregnancy jeopardizes the mother's life, the child is conceived through a rape or incest or if the child is severely handicapped. These hardships should not be minimized. But, as difficult (even tragic) as they may be, such circumstances do not justify killing an innocent human being.

Furthermore, thanks to modern medicine, situations where the life of the mother is truly at risk are extremely rare.

Direct abortion should be distinguished from indirect abortion, where an unborn child's death is an indirect consequence, and therefore unintentional, due to a necessary intervention to treat a dangerous medical condition. One such condition is the ectopic pregnancy, or "a tubal pregnancy," where the child implants and develops outside the uterus (usually the fallopian tube) and where there can be a serious threat to the mother's life.

Under the moral principle of "double effect," dangerously pathological maternal tissue of the fallopian tube can be removed as a threat to the mother's life, even if the tissue is also the location of the implanted fetus. The death of the fetus is an unfortunate and *unintended* (although foreseen) consequence of removing the diseased tissue.

Although certain principles can be stated regarding procedures addressing situations such as ectopic pregnancies, the moral evaluation of medical procedures in specific cases can differ. Consultation with a sound Catholic moralist and a medical doctor would be advised in this type of case.

Regarding rape or incest, statistics show the woman carrying the baby will much sooner forget the rape or incest than the abortion. Women know deep down that abortion is wrong. This is why so many women suffer depression and other psychological problems after abortions.

Regarding handicapped children, it is a very dangerous thing when individuals are allowed to decide
whether someone else should live simply because
that person is perceived to be of less value because
of a physical ailment. Since when is someone's value
determined by what they do or what they are like?
People with handicaps have much to offer society.
And even if the person is severely handicapped and
unable to function on his or her own, that person is
still a gift from God who can bring about tremendous love in the family if they are embraced and
viewed with the respect and value they deserve.

We should also be reminded that our Lord wants all
involved with the sin of abortion to seek forgiveness. Those who have had abortions are welcomed
with open arms if they turn back to God.

Question #150

"I know abortion is wrong, but how can I tell others why it is wrong?" Caitlin H., 15

A. There are two approaches you can take. The first
is to try to persuade people using moral principles
which we all generally accept. The second is to ap-
peal to revelation.

Begin with the idea that no one has the right to take
the life of an innocent person. Then discuss how
the baby is a separate human being, distinct from
his or her mother. Show how each child has its own

unique genetic identity, its own gender, its own heart-
beat and brain waves, eyes, hands, feet, etc. Challenge them to consider whether society is actually
going backwards, not forward, when it permits its
young to be killed to solve its problems. Acknowledge that women do have certain rights over their
bodies just as men do, but these rights (of both men
and women) are limited when they affect other
people's bodies. Abortion directly involves at least
two bodies, the mother's and her unborn child's.

Then discuss God. Mention the Bible teaches children are a gift from God and that God knows each
child from his or her first moment in the womb (Jer.
1:5, Is. 41:2, 44:24). Then ask, "Do you think God is
pleased that His precious gifts are being brutally killed
in the supposed safest place on earth — the mother's
womb?"

If people tell you not to bring religion into it, mention that *everything* is ultimately a religious issue.
God's law exists. You didn't make it up. You are just
telling what the law is.

Question #151

"Are you allowed to use birth control if you are a Catholic?" Kay B., 15

A. Your question is very important, but complicated,
so I will have to spend some time addressing it.

Does the Church allow birth control? It depends on what you mean by "birth control." Birth control, as the name suggests, regulates the birth of children. Consequently, birth control can include things such as contraception and abortion as well as Natural Family Planning (NFP).

Contraception is "any action which, either in anticipation of the conjugal act, or in its accomplishment, or in the development of its natural consequences, proposes, whether as an end or as a means, to render procreation impossible (*Humanae vitae*, no. 14). Abortion is the deliberate and direct ending of a pregnancy by terminating the life of an innocent, unborn child. Both are morally unacceptable means of "regulating birth" or "birth control," although abortion (and the forms of artificial contraception that can work as abortifacients) is the graver of the two immoral acts.

The sin of contraception may be committed by means of contraceptive pills, condoms, spermicides, physical or chemical "barriers," sterilization, etc. None of these are morally acceptable means of family planning.

On the other hand, there are morally acceptable means of "regulating births." Natural Family Planning (NFP) uses restriction of sexual intercourse to the infertile times of a woman's cycle to avoid pregnancy.

One of the most awesome gifts God gave man is the ability to generate new life made in God's image. Human beings are co-creators with God in that process. Contraception deliberately thwarts this God-given gift by treating conception as an evil thing to be avoided by physically or chemically altering the act of intercourse.

God designed sexual intercourse with two inherent "meanings." These meanings are sort of "written into" the act itself. They are the "unitive" or person-uniting meaning (loving) and the "procreative" or person-begetting meaning. These two meanings are interrelated and were intended by God to be present in every act of intercourse.

Every act of intercourse need not result in procreation. God designed things in such a way that this doesn't happen. But each act of intercourse should have, by its nature or the kind of act it is, the *possibility* of new life. The act should have a procreative meaning even if, here and now, procreation doesn't occur.

Contraception, as I've said, works against that meaning. It deprives the act of sexual intercourse of its procreative meaning. It turns it into another kind of act, one not only closed to new life but actually hostile to it. How so? By taking something like the pill, wearing something or otherwise doing something directly and intentionally opposed to new life.

Consider an analogy: Let's say I want to lose weight. One way is to avoid foods that have a lot of calories. But what if I ate large pieces of chocolate cake, savored the taste and swallowed it, but then, to avoid gaining weight, I made myself vomit? I enjoyed the goodness of the cake, but then did something, the unnatural act of forced vomiting, to avoid the consequences of my act.

The natural purpose of eating is for nourishing the body. Yes, it is pleasurable, but the pleasure that accompanies the act ought not to be our only purpose for eating. We ought not to eat in such a way that we actually thwart the nourishing purpose or "meaning" of eating, just for the pleasure of it. People who do that have an eating disorder.

Contraception is similar. People contracept to avoid a natural consequence of the sex act — conception — but still insist on the pleasure. In doing so, they attack one of the basic goods (new life) inherent in the act. And, not only do they hurt the procreative meaning of intercourse, they also attack its unitive or person-uniting (loving) meaning. People who contracept withhold a very important part of themselves in their love making: their power to generate with another a being *made in God's image*. They do not really give their whole selves to their spouse in intercourse; they do not fully become "one flesh"— in that sense.

We live in an age where children are often viewed with contempt. Children are often seen as burdens, liabilities and obstacles to "personal freedom." This is an anti-life mentality that too often manifests itself in families where parents are more concerned with material gain and leisure than raising up children for God. Sure, children are challenging to raise, but, ultimately, they bring far greater joy and love to the family than worldly pursuits.

Question #152

"Although Natural Family Planning isn't artificial like condoms and birth control pills, isn't birth control by its very nature unnatural?" Ernesto O., 17

A. Properly used, Natural Family Planning is not unnatural. But before we can see why, I should explain how NFP works.

Most women's ova are viable 12 to 24 hours. This means that pregnancy can only occur one to eight days a months, according to most fertility experts. NFP uses natural indicators (such as the presence of cervical mucus and its texture, changes in body temperature, etc.) in a woman's body to determine when she is fertile, and the likelihood that conception could occur. That means NFP can be used either to avoid conception or to increase the chances of conception by identifying when a women has ovulated.

Is there anything unnatural or morally wrong with a couple wanting to avoid pregnancy? Not necessarily. Although one of the essential purposes of marriage is the procreation of children, there may be circumstances (physical, social and even pyschological) where a couple may prudently avoid conceiving a child. Obviously, such circumstances should be serious, not frivolous. NFP *can* be abused, if a child is avoided for purely selfish reasons. But that is an abuse. In itself, NFP merely allows a couple to avoid intercourse during times when conception is possible. It is *non*-conceptive, not *contra*ceptive.

Nor is abstaining from sexual relations for good reasons unnatural. There might be all sorts of reasons for spouses to abstain — health, distance, time. Human beings have minds which God expects us to use. There is nothing wrong with using good judgement about when to have children and when to avoid doing so, provided that, if, despite our plans, children come anyway, we accept them as persons to be valued, rather than as burdens. It is not the planning of children that is the problem with contraception, but the anti-life, anti-procreative means that are employed.

NFP respects our human nature; it doesn't alter or thwart it as contraception does. NFP is not "natural" contraception. For contraception involves positively acting to alter the procreative nature of intercourse.

It takes an act that would otherwise be procreative (open to new life) and closes it by means of drugs, physical barriers or actions. Contraception *opposes* a natural outcome of intercourse: conception. NFP cooperates with nature, with the natural cycle of a woman's body. It may be used in a way to determine when sexual intercourse will be non-conceptive, but it doesn't alter the act of intercourse to make it anti-conceptive.

Question #153

"If you could not have children would it be OK to use artificial insemination and not adopt children?" Christine J., 16

A. Be sure to read my answer to the end because this is another one of those difficult questions that requires an openness to the explanations of and, ultimately, faith in the Church's authority on questions of faith and morality.

No, artificial insemination is not morally acceptable. Children should be "begotten, not made." Although parents who engage in artificial insemination may be well-intentioned, the means they choose to bring new life into existence is morally unacceptable. It amounts to manufacturing people by a technological process, rather than allowing human beings to be begotten by a truly human act of self-donating love (sexual intercourse).

Remember, for an act to be morally acceptable, the means (the way one does something) as well as the end (what a person wishes to achieve) must be morally good.

There is no doubt that a couple's inability to have children can be extremely painful and frustrating. But that doesn't make it OK to have a child through artificial insemination, anymore than it would make it OK to kidnap someone else's child because he or she already has 10 children. The end doesn't justify the means.

What about fertility drugs to help couples have children? The idea of using a drug to help fertility isn't, in itself, a moral problem. But there are some related issues that can be, so the matter needs to be carefully thought through and all the health risks considered, both to the mother and her potential offspring.

For example, sometimes fertility drugs result in the conception of multiple pre-born children. Not just twins or triplets, but even quintuplets, septuplets, etc. To diminish health risks to the mother or to some of children in the womb, doctors may propose "selective terminations"— abortions, in other words, of some of the embryonic babies. That is not morally acceptable; it amounts to unjustly killing innocent human beings. Imagine how you would feel knowing that your little brother or sister was "selectively terminated" and that it might just as well have been you?

Although this may be difficult to accept, God may have allowed certain couples to be infertile to challenge them to open their hearts to adoption. There are countless children here and abroad in need of loving parents. Adoption is a better, more loving and generous choice than artificial insemination.

Question #154

"Is dating OK?" Danny N., 14

A. Of course, if done with respect for God's laws and for the person you are dating. Healthy dating can lead to healthy and stable marriages.

Although chaste dating for the mere fun of companionship is acceptable, it's important to remember that *marriage* is the primary goal of dating. Healthy marriages are the bedrock to a healthy and stable society. In addition, dating offers a chance to develop interpersonal skills, which will be helpful in married life or should you choose a religious vocation.

Society's influence, especially television's, forces people to think they are weird or incomplete if they are not in a "hot and heavy" dating relationship. This is a lie. The "emotional charge" dating gives is not the primary purpose for dating. Finding a marriage partner is the primary purpose. This is why it's so important to be prudent in our dating choices and perspectives.

Although I said that dating can develop social skills, there are other ways to do this. You don't have to worry you'll be weird if you don't date a lot (or at all). Also, one should not be forced into dating someone you do not want to or *before* you truly want to.

Question #155

"How old do you have to be to date if you're a Catholic?" Kay B., 15

A. There is no specific age but, in my opinion, a Catholic who is serious about his or her Faith should probably wait at least until the late high school years before casually dating. Some would even say a person should wait until the late college years. There's too much to accomplish and focus on in your high school and college years. Teenagers have their whole lives ahead of them for dating relationships.

In addition, a teenager goes through many physical changes which can be confusing. He or she doesn't need the added stress that comes with even good dating relationships, let alone the bad ones.

Question #156

"Is there hope for a young Catholic to find a good Catholic spouse in this society?" Ed H., 18

A. You sound like a young man who is trying to live a virtuous life. Yes, there are surely tens of thousands young ladies who are also trying to live a virtuous life. You may have to hang around the right venues to find them, such as church, a youth or young adult group, a college Newman center or even a respected Catholic dating service.

My advice is to stay strong, have faith and pray a novena to St. Raphael, who is a patron saint of finding that special someone. You should also pray for discernment about what your true vocation is. You may be destined to marry the most wonderful bride of all, the Church, as a priest.

Question #157

"Is it OK to date a non-Catholic?" Nicollete C., 16

A. It is certainly not impossible to find "Mr. or Mrs. Right" in another faith. However, a mutual outlook on life, which most clearly comes from a shared Catholic Faith, is almost vital to a successful dating relationship and marriage.

The primary goal of dating is to find a suitable marriage partner. Good marriages most often come from healthy dating relationships. We should not date merely to satisfy some emotional or physical need.

While a successful marriage between a Catholic and non-Catholic Christian (or even a non-Christian) is not impossible, such marriages bring with them special challenges and unique dangers. Marriage requires hard work. It will be even harder if there are religious differences. Scripture speaks of binding yourself to someone who is on the same spiritual level as you. "Do not be yoked (mated) with those who are different, with an unbeliever. For what partnership do righteousness and lawlessness have" (2 Cor. 6:14)?

That is why the Church generally encourages Catholics to marry other Catholics and why you should be careful about dating non-Catholics.

Question #158

"Why is my dad so strict against my going out with non-Catholic boys?" Patti H., 16

A. Your father knows that casual dating often leads to serious dating. And serious dating is part of the process by which we find our future spouses. No doubt he would prefer you to marry a Catholic boy. He believes the Catholic Faith and would like his daughter to marry someone who does, too. He knows a couple who shares the same faith will be better prepared to handle the challenges all marriages face. So he is really looking out for your happiness.

Question #159

"In a relationship, how far is 'too far' before it is considered a sin?" Jolene N., 17

A. We are made in the image and likeness of God, which means we cannot treat another person as an object of pleasure. Therefore, actions that directly stimulate sexual passion (like touching another's sexual organs) are not morally justifiable. Our sexual gifts have a much higher and special purpose.

Actions like holding hands, modest kisses and embraces are perfectly fine as long as you have a firm presence of mind that these *modest* acts will not lead to serious sins against chastity. Sins against chastity are sins against the Sixth Commandment.

Loose sexual behavior becomes a tyrant that keeps making more demands on those involved. Eventually, you and your date will get bored with just kissing and will want to move on to other things. This is called the "law of declining returns." Kissing doesn't always give the same excitement as when you first did it. The more one feeds these passions, the more your will becomes weakened.

Also, because guys tend to be more physically oriented than girls, they often stop doing the healthy and morally acceptable things they used to do with their dates. Activities like going to the mall or movies seem to go by the wayside once the two become sexually active.

Deep kissing and embracing may be somewhat justifiable after there is a formal engagement but, even then, the two people should be cautious.

Question #160

"Is French kissing OK?" Josh M., 13

A. Although it's exciting, passionate kissing or embracing out of a mere general sex interest is a near occasion of sin, perhaps venially sinful, but not in and of itself a mortal sin. It's a near occasion of sin because it can easily lead to greater sin.

Two unmarried people should avoid getting "hot and heavy" with deep kissing because this almost always leads to more serious actions.

Here's an analogy: Let's say you were driving in a 3-ton truck with a 600 lb. piano on the back down a steep hill. Would you first put on the brakes 10 feet before the intersection? Certainly not. You would start to put on the brakes at the top of the hill and ease the truck and piano down the hill. The same prudence should guide our dating relationships. Take them slow.

A modest kiss or embrace is perfectly fine, but beware of getting too physically intimate. It will only make things harder in the end and may take you down a road you really don't want to travel at this point in your life.

Today's teens should not be preoccupied with dating as much as they are. They should focus on schooling, extracurricular activities like sports or drama and developing skills for a future career. I know chaste dating can be difficult at times, but you can do it if you practice virtue and seek God's grace.

Question #161

"Why is there so much sex going on with teens today as compared to when my parents were young?" Daniel N., 17

A. I'm guessing based on your age that your parents spent their teenage years in the 1960's or early '70s. And, quite frankly, those were the years that started much of the mess we have today. Unfortunately, things have gotten worse. There are some concrete reasons why teens are so much more sexually active today than in years past.

The number one reason why teens are having more premarital sex is because Satan is working overtime. It's important to remember that any sinful act is ultimately prompted by the workings of Satan, who desires that we lose our soul.

The second biggest reason is due to the invention of artificial birth control. Those who grew up before birth control was widespread had the same sexual urges, but had a tremendous fear of unwed pregnancy because of the stigma that went along with it. Contraception misleads people into thinking they needn't fear unwanted pregnancy or sexually transmitted disease, not to mention the harmful psychological effects of sexual intimacy on unmarried people; thus contraception actually encourages premarital sex.

A third factor is the decline in morals throughout society. Much of society, especially the media, has little concern for modesty. In fact, a study in the 1980s by researcher Sheila Fletcher concluded that the average teenager will view over 9,000 sex acts (or implied sex) acts on television *every year!* Over 80 percent of these sex acts are done outside of the marriage context. *And that was in the 1980s.* Most would agree things have gotten worse in recent years.

Also, the bad results of premarital sex are almost never portrayed on television. The stars of the popular TV shows never seem to have broken hearts, get pregnant, suffer hemorrhages from abortions or suffer the horrible effects of a sexually transmitted disease. They seem to have wonderful lives. This, of course, is not reality. Thousands of these tragedies occur *every day* to people as a result of premarital sex.

There are many other reasons why more teens are having sex today than in years past, including earlier dating, more broken homes which cause loneliness and a greater search for intimacy, and increasing peer pressure. If you're interested in more on this topic, refer to the books *Why Wait?* by Josh McDowell and Dick Day and *Real Love* by Mary Beth Bonacci. I have listed them in the "Resources" section at the end of the book.

Question #162

"Is having sex before getting married a sin?" John H., 14

A. This is an important answer so I ask that you take your time to read it completely.

Yes, premarital sex is a sin. Unfortunately, too many young people have not been taught the reasons why sex outside marriage is wrong, so many have fallen into this lifestyle. It is my hope that because of their ignorance, today's teens may be judged by an easier standard, but, of course, there's no guarantee that this will be the case.

Regarding teen sexuality, I believe if you have clear answers about *why* God says we are to remain chaste, you will be better equipped to save the precious gift of your sexuality for its proper use and time.

As you know, God invented sex. And, because God

invented sex, we know that it is a good thing! Anything that God makes or institutes is good because He is good. However, with this good thing come certain stipulations. Why? Because God doesn't want the good thing to become a source of pain, evil, selfishness, or death. He wants sex to be the absolute profound and wonderful act it was meant to be. He gave us the sexual attraction to bring the two sexes together in a way that would lead to marriage and procreation, which is the *ultimate* (not the only, but ultimate) purpose of marriage.

Think about it. God could have brought new humans into the world by another means. He might have established a world in which He was the *sole* creator of the human person, body and soul (without human interaction). He can do what He wants — He's God. The male/female relationship could have been just a platonic friendship. But no, God established a system of reproduction that included humans. He chose the sexual act as the means by which the creation of humans, who would be endowed with an invaluable soul, would be achieved.

The soul of the new baby will last for all eternity. Because the human person, especially the soul, is so valuable and important, the sexual act *must* be important. And, like most important things, it's logical to think it has a proper and improper use.

Besides the tremendous pain, selfishness and evil

that can come with sex outside of marriage (including broken hearts, abortion, diseases, hardened hearts and low self-esteem), it can easily lead to unwed pregnancies. Unwed pregnancies lead to all sorts of problems, especially for the female. Almost all government and private studies show that unwed pregnancies lead to a cycle of poverty, illiteracy, abuse, maladjusted children, emotional disturbances, like a desperate search for intimacy, and much more. There are exceptions to this, but they are few.

Although it can be a good thing for the couple to get married if the girl gets pregnant, there can be risk as well. There is a 60 percent chance that they will get divorced, according to a study in *People* magazine.

When two people bare their bodies to each other, they also bare their souls. They implicitly say to each other, "I am exclusively yours and you are exclusively mine...And I will never leave you or hurt you." Yet, this rarely ends up being the case. Too many relationships end up with heartbreaks, pain, a physical side effect and even a loss of religious faith. With premarital sex, one has almost everything to lose and very little to gain.

The sexual act between two people is the most intimate expression of human love possible. It really only makes sense when it is consummated in a committed life-long relationship.

Question #163

"Is it OK to have sex before you are married if you are going to be with that person forever?" Shelley T., 14

A. Before I answer your question, let me show you two actual letters people wrote to columnist Ann Landers that I found in the book *Why Wait?*, which I mentioned earlier. They say a lot. The first was written by a women:

> I met him; I liked him.
> I liked him; I loved him
> I loved him; I let him
> *I let him; I lost him.*

The second was written by a man:

> I saw her.
> I liked her.
> I loved her.
> I wanted her.
> I asked her.
> *She said no.*
> I married her.
> After sixty years,
> I still have her.

No good intention (love/marriage) ever justifies doing an evil (premarital sex). For example, we could not sell drugs to raise money for the poor because we don't know what evil may result from the drug selling. Doing an evil act is like shooting a gun in public; you never know if the stray bullet will affect someone. Likewise, you never know what problems will result from breaking a very clear Commandment of God.

The Bible is very clear on the spiritual fate of those who sin against God (and their own bodies) through premarital sex *and who do not repent before they die.* "Do not be deceived; neither fornicators, nor idolaters, nor adulterers, nor boy prostitutes, nor practicing homosexuals... will inherit the kingdom of God" (1 Cor. 6:9-10).

We also read: "Avoid (sexual) immorality. Every other sin a person commits is outside the body, but the immoral person sins against his own body. Do you not know that your body is the temple of the Holy Spirit within you, whom you have from God? For you have been purchased at a price. Therefore, glorify God in your body" (1 Cor. 6:18-20).

Jesus' death on the cross opened up the gates of heaven and gave us the hope of eternal life. He purchased us at a great price. It is a slap in the face of Jesus to flagrantly disregard His Commandments and make up our own religious and moral beliefs.

Lastly, the overwhelming percentage of teenage relationships break up after short periods of time. While
you may believe that you will be with your boyfriend all your life, there are no guarantees. In fact, a
recent study by author Michael McManus showed
that only 15 percent of couples who lived together
before marriage stayed together. Also, couples who
abstained from sex before marriage were up to 47
percent more satisfied with their marital relationships
than those who slept together before marriage. *Although these may not match your situation exactly,
they convey powerful points you should consider.*

When sex is introduced into a dating relationship,
things start to change almost immediately. The two
people, especially the girl, become anxious and preoccupied with worries about the relationship. The
relationship occupies too much of one's time. It affects one's schooling, friends and family relationships, self-esteem and relationship with God.

Question #164

**"If you love the person, I don't think it
should matter if you have sex before you
are married." Jeanette C., 15**

A. True love involves sacrifice. It also involves *fidel-
ity*, which means faithfulness. Think about it. If you
and your boyfriend are not faithful to God's laws,
what evidence is there that you will be faithful to
each other?

I used to tell the girls in my youth group: "If a guy will not sacrifice for you and is willing to subject you to the many problems that come with premarital sex, then he doesn't *really* love you. He may be infatuated with you. He may have great fun with you. But he doesn't *truly* love you. True love is much different."

The definition of love is "to want what is best for the other simply because it is best for that person" (and not because you will get something out of it). Can a boy *really* say he loves a girl if he is willing to subject her to physical danger (early pregnancy, side effects of birth control) and the emotional stress (heartache, anxiousness) of a sexual relationship? And what about the spiritual dangers? Can you imagine a boyfriend saying, "I love you, so let's risk going to hell together?" I don't think someone who *really* loves you would subject you to this risk.

Love is based on friendship, and a friendship is really not a good one if (1) it leads to sin, (2) it troubles one's conscience, (3) lowers one's ideals and (4) weakens one's faith.

If two people really love each other, they'll want the relationship to last. I challenge young teens who are dating to treat the person like a brother or sister in Christ — because that's what they are. They are *literally* God's adopted son or daughter — like you are.

This makes you their spiritual brother or sister. Would you do something evil to one of God's children?

Unmarried couples should show modest affection. If a couple is already sexually active, they should stop the sexual activity *and remains chaste until marriage*. If they do, they stand a much better chance of not breaking up and avoiding marriage problems later on.

Question #165

"Besides diseases and getting a girl pregnant, how can having premarital sex affect you negatively if you love the girl, she loves you and you are mentally ready, like those in my age group?" Peter C., 17

A. Sexual activity is such an important and powerful act (because it is the means by which God brings new souls into the world) that no unmarried person can *really* handle it, especially a teenager. Why? Because no one can *really* handle sin.

Sin is a creation of Satan. He has far more intellect and energy than we do. He is a pure spirit who is not subject to the limitations of the body.

Also, if "diseases" and "getting a girl pregnant" aren't enough reasons, I'm not sure I'll be able to satisfy you at all. Nevertheless, here are 15 other reasons to save sex for marriage:

1) Premarital sex inhibits your ability to love truly. Sex can be a real obstacle to developing healthy relationships, especially for men. Men tend to focus very much on the physical pleasure of the relationship. Men need to *learn* how to love and communicate. It's not uncommon for a guy to stop communicating, bringing flowers or talking sweet once he becomes sexually active with a girl. Premarital sex stifles one's ability to communicate.

2) It makes people selfish. Because a teenage pregnancy (and the difficulties that come with it) may result, premarital sex is a very selfish thing for two people to do. You are putting a baby's future in jeopardy because of the problems that most young married teens face. Low-paying jobs and receiving welfare are much more common in young marriages. And, children that are raised in these situations suffer the consequences of the unstable home. So, it's selfish to think of one's own pleasure and disregard that the act might hurt another later.

3) Preoccupies your mind. Young people should be worrying about the next math test, not the next pregnancy test. I've seen young girls and guys who were fervent about life get all their energy "zapped" out of them after they become sexually active. Why? Premarital sex can become "all consuming." Once one is sexually active, it can constantly occupy one's thoughts. Girls become more anxious with thoughts

of guilt and low self-worth and guys get consumed
with the thought of repeating the act.

4) Broken hearts. Think about how many guys and
girls have had crushed hearts after a break-up, especially when they see their "ex" with another person.
Sex creates a bond between people. When the bond
is broken due to a break-up, hearts can be torn in
two. Scientists may have invented a condom that
can prevent pregnancy, but no scientists will ever
invent a condom to protect against a broken heart.

5) Guilt. Premarital sex is sort of like stealing. You
know you are taking what really isn't yours. Uncon-
fessed sin and the guilt that comes with premarital
sex causes all kinds of problems, including mild
neurosis and the hardening of one's heart. Living a
chaste life makes you feel liberated.

*6) Premarital sex can make you marry the wrong
person.* Sex is powerful. It creates a bond between
two people. A sexually active relationship can cause
a blindness in one or both parties. You may fall in
love with a person who is bad for you.

7) It's really a lie to the other person. Two people say
with their bodies, "I give my whole self to you." But
in reality they haven't done that or they would be
married. Even if a couple is engaged they haven't
really promised themselves wholly and exclusively

to one another. They've only *promised* to promise. Before marriage, sex between them would be a grave deceit, for they really wouldn't (and couldn't) mean what they say by their actions.

8) Causes future jealousies. Both men and women can suffer flashbacks or jealous pangs at the thought of their spouse or "significant other" being intimate with someone else.

9) Sexual dissatisfaction once one is married. When a person gets married to someone after being sexually active with others, there is a greater chance they will be dissatisfied with the marital love life because they will most likely compare it to past experiences. Whereas, a person who has not engaged in sexual activity will appreciate his spouse and their love life much more.

10) You only have one "first time." Wouldn't sex be much nicer if you were to wait until your honeymoon? After being chaste with your wife during your courtship, the reward is much greater.

11) Avoid awkwardness and tension. Nervously fornicating in the back seat of the car or in your parent's basement does not compare to the true peace that comes from *knowing* you and your spouse have a clear conscience because God has blessed your union in marriage.

12) Sexual addictions or problems. Again, sex is a powerful thing. Most people cannot handle premarital sex. Subsequently, addictions and perversions can develop.

13) It can lead to a lack of trust of the opposite sex. A relationship that "goes sour" can stay with someone all their life and can affect that person's next relationship. People who've felt "used" by others have a problem trusting. This can lead to divorce, which can bring about a whole host of problems, especially for the children.

14) You're jeopardizing your salvation. God is very clear on the topic. Sex is His gift for the *married* couple. God said it, so that should settle it. Unfortunately, the world is pushing God's teachings out of society. People, especially the young, are not being taught these profound truths. Subsequently, many will risk losing their souls if they live unchaste lives and do not repent before death.

15) Leading another astray. OK, let's say you repent and get saved. But what if the girl or boy you introduced to sex in high school never turns back? And, what if you were partly the cause of that person's path of destruction? Are you ready to stand before Jesus with that on your conscience?

In addition to "pregnancy" and "diseases," these 15

statements should give you more than enough reasons to save sex for marriage.

Question #166

"There's a lot of sexual temptation out there. How can a person survive until marriage?" Dennis S., 18

A. Here are 10 ways you can have healthy dating
relationships and remain chaste. Several of them are
from the books, *Why Wait?* and *Real Love,* which I
mentioned earlier.

1) *Pray.* Talk to Jesus. Also ask for the prayers of the
saints, especially St. Maria Goretti, who is the patron
saint for those who desire to be chaste.

2) *Say three "Hail Mary's" every day for purity.* If
you ask, Our Lady will pray for you to God and help
keep you pure.

3) *Frequent the Sacraments.* Jesus gave us the seven
Sacraments to give us supernatural help.

4) *Know that you are not alone.* There are many
others teens who also believe that being chaste is a
better way to live.

5) *Set high standards.* The person who stands for
nothing falls for everything. So set high standards.

6) Have the courage to leave bad relationships. Do not stay in a relationship that is causing you to sin.

7) Value the other person. Remember the guy or girl you are thinking of being sexually active with is someone's future husband or wife. Would you want someone fooling around with your future spouse? If not, then you should not be fooling around with someone else's future spouse.

8) Have someone to talk to. If your parents are not available, speak to a priest, sibling or youth minister with whom you feel comfortable and who is supportive of Church teaching.

9) Date responsibly. Set goals, time limits and specific dating plans. Also consider dating in large groups or with at least one other couple so you don't get into a dangerous situation.

10) Pray with your date. Wouldn't that be cool? At the very least, say a private prayer before the date.

If you have already engaged in premarital sex, you can become a "second-time virgin." You won't get your physical virginity back, but you *can* make a commitment from this day forth to wait until you are married. Would you never save money again if you spent all that was in your savings account? Of course not. The same applies to premarital sex. If you made a mistake, get back up and vow not to make the same mistake again.

Question #167

"Is masturbation a sin? If so, why?" Name and age withheld

A. Yes, masturbation is a sin because our sexual organs are not playthings for self-gratification. They are intended for sexual relations between spouses, to express and share mutual, self-donating love and for the procreation of children. When we use our sexual power of loving and procreating according to God's purpose, we honor Him and our bodies. When we don't, we dishonor God and our bodies, which Scripture condemns (Rom. 1:24). Masturbation is often called "self-abuse" precisely because the person who masturbates abuses his body.

Masturbation is also unnatural, which makes it a sin against nature — which was designed and given order by God. It is pleasure alone that becomes the end goal. not the joy found in doing something truly loving.

Masturbation is also very dangerous to one's social and interpersonal skills because it is a selfish act that turns the person inward. It makes one self-absorbed. Masturbation can also make someone a selfish spouse who is only concerned about his or her own sexual pleasure. This, of course, could be harmful to marriage.

There are many faithful priests who will say that, although the act is objectively (fundamentally) sinful, the subjective (personal) guilt of someone today *may* not be present due to immaturity, the widespread sexual messages in the media and the lack of proper catechetical formation of today's youth. *This should not, however, give someone license to sin.* Masturbation is sinful. If someone has a problem with this sin, I recommend the person find a priest with whom he or she feels comfortable and ask for spiritual direction.

Question #168
"Is pornography wrong?" Clark K., 14

A. Yes, it is sinful for a few reasons. The first reason is because it fosters impure thoughts, which are a sin against the Ninth Commandment. Second, it easily leads to impure actions such as masturbation, fornication and adultery. Third, it can bring about a desire for unnatural sex because much of pornography presents a warped view of the sexual act.

According to a study done at the University of Utah, pornography results in the following: (1) It stimulates and arouses aggressive sexual feelings. (2) It shows and instructs in detail how to do the act. (3) It legitimizes the act through repeated exposure. And, (4) it increases the likelihood the viewer will act out what he or she sees.

Another study at New York University showed that repeated viewing of pornography leads to an increase in rape. Serial killers Ted Bundy and Jeffrey Dahmer stated that their addiction to pornography contributed to their dehumanization of their victims. This made killing their victims much easier. Some have said that pornography can be as addictive as some of the most potent drugs.

Pornography deadens the senses. It reduces the opposite sex to a mere object of pleasure. It also stifles one's ability to communicate, which will be very harmful to a future dating relationship or marriage.

Question #169

"What should you do if you try 'second-time virginity' as chastity speakers have suggested, but you end up being sexually active again?" Clare H., 14

A. Go to Confession to be reconciled with God and then try harder. The "second-time virginity" plan should not be viewed as a license to sin again and again. You should *really* do your best to avoid this serious sin. It is a grave offense against the Commandments. If you do fall, get up quickly and reconcile yourself to God, the Church and, if possible, the person with whom you sinned.

You should also examine your conscience to see if you were really trying to avoid the near occasion of sin. If not, be more diligent. Also speak to a priest, youth minister or Christian counselor about the situation. They should be able to offer advice on how you can strengthen your walk with the Lord.

Question #170

"Is virginity on the rise or are all teenagers 'doing it?'" Ed H., 18

A. Among religious teens, there is definitely a trend towards chastity. Many new movements in Catholic, Protestant and other religious circles have started in recent years. Young people are seeing that it is truly cool and even heroic to live a chaste life. They like being different. (It's unfortunate that nowadays a person is considered "different" if he or she is chaste.) Young people are seeing the real peace of mind and heart that comes from living a faithful Christian life.

Regarding teens as a whole, I would say that things are probably getting worse. Without God, things will always get worse. There are many teens who abstain from sex because of the fear of sexually transmitted diseases, but many of them will eventually believe the "safe sex" lie and this will then lead to sexual activity.

Don't give up though. Even if you are the only one left (which you'll never be), you will still be right. You will still be the one who ultimately has peace of mind and conscience.

Question #171

"Why is being 'gay' a sin?" Philip T., 15

A. There's a difference between the homosexual orientation (finding members of the same gender sexually attractive) and homosexual acts (sexual activity between members of the same sex). The Church doesn't say that the mere homosexual *orientation* is a sin — though it is an inclination or a tendency toward sinful behavior that must be resisted. But homosexual *acts* are always sinful, because sexual acts are intended by God for husbands and wives not unmarried persons, whether the same or opposite sex.

People with a homosexual orientation (like unmarried people with a heterosexual orientation) must learn self-control and chastity. All unmarried people, whether homosexual or heterosexual, should develop virtue, rely on God's grace to live morally and avoid situations which will cause temptation to sin.

The Church officially teaches in its document *On the Pastoral Care of Homosexual Persons* that homosexual acts are "intrinsically disordered" and that "special concern and pastoral attention should be directed toward those who have this condition, lest they be led to believe that the living out of this orientation in homosexual activity is a morally acceptable option. It is not" (Article #3).

Scripture condemns homosexual activity: "Therefore, God handed them to their degrading passions. Their females exchanged natural relations for unnatural, and the males likewise gave up natural relations with females and burned with lust for one another. Males did shameful things with one another and thus received in their own persons the due penalty for their perversity" (Rom. 1:26-27). Other verses include: Lev. 18:22 and 20:13; Gen. 18:20; 1 Cor. 6:9.

There are factors which can diminish a person's blameworthiness for homosexual acts, although nothing can ever make homosexual acts morally acceptable.

Homosexual acts also violate the moral law. The Bible teaches that the sexual difference between men and women is divinely willed (Gen. 1:27-28; 2:24; 5:2). Man and woman are to become one flesh. This means more than just the sexual act. It also means the natural end result of sexual activity — a baby. A baby is the direct result of the two becoming one. It has aspects of both the father and mother in its makeup. Homosexual sex could never result in a baby. It can never fully achieve the "one flesh" that our sexual power is intended to achieve. Therefore, the moral law, which is written by God, implicitly condemns homosexual activity.

Pastoral care and compassion should be extended to those suffering from homosexual tendencies. Those interested in more information should read *The Truth About Homosexuality* by Father John Harvey, which is listed in the "Resources" section.

Question #172

"If we are supposed to accept others as they are, why does the Church try to change homosexuals?" Jody G., 16

A. We are supposed to love everyone, but if someone is sinning we are not only *allowed* to call them to repentance, but are actually *required* to do so.

St. James says if we lead someone to the truth we not only assist in their salvation, but in our own as well (James 5:19). Helping someone leave the homosexual lifestyle is actually a great act of charity for two reasons: (1) You are leading them from a lifestyle that is spiritually dangerous. The Bible clearly states that practicing homosexuals will not inherit the kingdom of God (1 Cor. 6:9). (2) Homosexuality is also physically dangerous. According to the American Family Association, male homosexuals have an average life span of just 39 years. And, this is due to more than just the AIDS epidemic. The life span for homosexual women is just a few years more than their male counterparts. Both also have much higher rates of sickness, suicide, alcoholism and depression. And, in locations where homosexuality is more widely accepted, the numbers are actually higher. This refutes the notion that the mental problems of the homosexual are caused by society's condemnation of the lifestyle.

So, any effort on the part of people in the Church to help homosexuals lead chaste lives is an act of love on the part of the Church.

Question #173

"If gay people are sinners, should we hate them?" Tom S., 14

A. Jesus said, "Let the one among you who is without sin cast the first stone" (John 8:7). If we are supposed to hate and, even, kick out members of the Church who sin, there would be no one left. We all sin to a greater or lesser degree. Be thankful there is forgiveness. Scripture also says, "But if you do not forgive others, neither will the Father forgive your trespasses" (Matt. 6:15).

We're supposed to hate the sin, but not the sinner. We are allowed to bring sin to someone's attention, and call them to repentance, but this is to be done in a spirit of love and humility.

Question #174

"If being a lesbian or being gay is wrong, why did God make people this way?" Luis C., 14

A. God *permits* some people to have a homosexual orientation, but this doesn't mean God created them that way or wants people to engage in homosexual acts. God also permits some people to have leukemia or schizophrenia. Does that mean these things are good in themselves? The fact is that we live in a world damaged by sin. God is correcting that through the teachings and sanctification offered by Christ through the Church. But He allows bad things to continue for a time in order to bring an even greater good from them.

God can use things like physical sickness or mental illness or conditions like, say, anorexia or homosexuality as means of growing in holiness. Yet that doesn't make them good in themselves. The schizophrenic person cannot say, "God made me this way, therefore I can do whatever I want." Similarly, the homosexual person can't reasonably argue, "I am this way. God made me this way, therefore I can act on my orientation."

Many of us find strong tendencies in ourselves, sexual or otherwise, to act in certain ways. Imagine what would happen if we decided to act on these impulses using the "God-made-this-way-so-I-can-act-this-way logic"of some homosexual activists? Almost anything could be justified. The alcoholic, the petty thief or even the child molester could excuse everything with: "God made me like this."

You should also know there is no valid scientific evidence that God made homosexuals with that condition. The studies which are often cited have been found to have fundamental problems. Most Christian and non-Christian psychologists agree the disorder is not chosen by the homosexual person. However, there is considerable evidence that homosexual orientation develops because of situations in early childhood.

Dr. Joseph Nicolosi, a Los Angeles-based psychologist, has found excellent success in assisting homosexuals rediscover their true heterosexual identity through "reparative therapy," which is a form of counseling that addresses past disturbances in the emotional and psychological formation of young children. His work is detailed in his book *Healing the Homosexual.*

Also, Dr. Elizabeth Moberly, a British psychologist, maintains that homosexual behavior is due to difficulties in parent-child relationships. Her study is examined in Father John Harvey's book, *The Homosexual Person.* Both Father Harvey and Dr. Nicolosi have been ridiculed by the homosexual community, secular psychology and the secular media because of their studies and implications. Nevertheless, their research is quite sound. Their books are listed in the "Resources" at the end of this book.

A homosexual person who struggles to be chaste, depends on God and lives a holy life can see his or her sexual problem as something permitted by God, without inferring that homosexuality is good in itself or that homosexual acts are moral. As is the case with any serious affliction, it can be the means to holiness if one turns to God and relies on Him.

Question #175

"Will God accept you if you are gay?" Nicole W., 14

A. Certainly, if the homosexual person lives a chaste life and does not act on his or her orientation. In fact, if homosexuals remain chaste, they will surely store up heavenly treasures due to the difficulties they face. A chaste homosexual is truly heroic, especially in this age where the lifestyle is so widely promoted.

God is love, so in that sense He "accepts" everybody, although He doesn't accept everything they do. The real question is, will *we* accept *God?* Will we accept His love for us, even if that means giving up whatever sinful lifestyle we have chosen?

The pressure to abandon God's laws is certainly great. We should offer anyone struggling with this cross our prayers and support. You may consider directing them to Father John Harvey's ministry, Courage, or Dr. Joseph Nicolosi's Thomas Aquinas Psychological Clinic, in Los Angeles, Calif. Both ministries have found good results in helping the homosexual person rediscover his or her true heterosexuality. I've listed them in the "Resources" section.

Question #176

"I think I am gay. What should I do?" Adam T., 15

A. Pray and seek solid Catholic counseling from someone who supports the Church's teaching on the subject. Otherwise, you may be given false information. There are many young people, especially boys, who wonder about their sexual orientation. This can be caused by developmental obstacles in the first few years of age.

I recommend you call one of the two ministries listed in the "Resources" section who are dedicated to assisting the person struggling with homosexuality. You will find peace and direction once you understand the cause of the problem and are given a plan of action to work on. I have seen it work in a friend's life and know of a few others who have be helped from counseling.

Question #177

"Is bisexuality OK?" Justin B., 15

A. No, bisexuality involves homosexual acts, which are condemned in Scripture (Lev. 18:22, 20:13, Gen. 18:20, 1 Cor. 6:9). Bisexuality is contrary to the monogamous and heterosexual lifestyle set forth by God. Bisexuality has become "fashionable" in recent years. This is due to the breakdown of stable family structures, insidious information on television and in the movies, a lack of good moral formation in our schools and a general breakdown in morals in society.

Scripture speaks of how lust in man's heart will lead to degrading practices (Rom. 1:26-27). Sin fuels more sin. There is no limit to where the sinful human heart can lead. Bisexuality is no more acceptable than homosexuality.

Question #178

"Is it true that the only unforgivable sin is suicide?" Ellie M., 17

A. The only unforgivable sin is the sin against the Holy Spirit. And that is the sin of the final impenitence, which is a final refusal to repent and accept God's grace. The Pharisees sinned against the Holy Spirit because they refused to repent, hence, they could not be forgiven (CCC #864).

Suicide is in itself gravely sinful. Human life is a

precious gift of God, and the Commandment, "You shall not kill," applies to killing ourselves as well as others. Suicide contradicts the natural inclination of the human being to preserve and perpetuate life. It is gravely contrary to the just love of self, according to the Catechism (CCC #2281). If one freely chooses to commit suicide with sufficient reflection and deliberation, knowing it to be gravely sinful, he sins mortally.

Even so, many (if not most) people who commit suicide may not knowingly and freely be doing something they understand to be gravely sinful. Severe psychological factors may enter into the situation. These can diminish the responsibility of the one committing suicide (CCC #2282).

Also, we should never underestimate God's saving grace. For example, it is said that Jesus appeared to St. Catherine of Siena to tell her that her brother, who committed suicide by jumping from a bridge, had repented before he hit the water. Granted, this story is not a doctrine of the Church, but it offers some hope for the families of those who have committed suicide.

On the issue of suicide, the *Catechism* closes by saying that we should not despair of the eternal salvation of persons who have taken their own lives. By ways known by God alone, He can provide an opportunity for repentance (CCC #2283).

Question #179

"What is the Church's view on the death penalty?" John C., 15

A. Here's the short answer: The Church allows the state the right to use capital punishment, but strongly discourages its use except in very rare occasions because other, bloodless, means are usually sufficient to protect society. Also, the death penalty tends to contribute to the cheapening of human life throughout society (CCC #2266 & 2267).

Here's the longer answer: The Church has a long-standing tradition which allows the state the right to inflict the death penalty to protect the common good, but the state is not obliged to do so. Biblical passages support the use of the death penalty. The passages include Genesis 9:6 ("If anyone sheds the blood of man, by man shall his blood be shed."), Gen. 21:23 ("an eye for an eye") and Romans 13:4 ("The ruler...does not bear the sword without purpose. It is the servant of God to inflict wrath on the evil doer.")

In recent years, however, some popes, including John Paul II and many American bishops, have spoken against the use of the death penalty. They offer several reasons including: (1) that it is not a deterrent, (2) the state may run the risk of killing an innocent person, (3) it may prevent the conversion of the convicted, (4) it seems to be exercised on a disproportionate number of minorities and low-income people, and (5) it further erodes society's respect for life.

Modern-day Church leaders believe that because morals continue to decline and methods of incarceration today better protect the public, we should strive to eliminate capital punishment. Reflecting on Jesus' condemnation of revenge and His call to "turn the other cheek" (Matt. 5:39), we should value all life, including the criminal's, and, where possible, seek to reform the sinner and convert his heart to the loving God.

Question #180

"In the Bible, it says 'eye for an eye, tooth for a tooth, etc.' This being so, why is the Church against the death penalty if the person had committed murder?" Jody G., 16

A. The Church is not against capital punishment in every instance. If bloodless means are not available or not sufficient to secure the protection of society from murderers then the state can exercise its fundamental right to administer capital punishment to safeguard society.

Regarding the verse you cited, many orthodox Catholic theologians believe that this is a law of the Old Testament which was superseded with the coming of Christ and the New Covenant. They cite the verse where Jesus commands us to "turn the other cheek"

(Matt. 5:39) and the verse which says that if a man lives by the sword, he will perish by the sword (Matt. 26:52) as evidence that the "eye for an eye" principle no longer generally applies.

In any event, the Church asks that capital punishment be used in very rare situations because it may endanger society's respect for the dignity of the human person, who is made in the image and likeness of God. The death penalty can perpetuate the culture of death.

Question #181

"Will you go to hell if you are forced to fight for your country in a war and, subsequently, kill someone?" Adrian A., 15

A. No. Fighting for your country if it is a "just war" is a noble thing to do and, unfortunately, the death of men and women is a natural consequence of war. However, if your superiors order you to do something that is intrinsically immoral, like executing innocent victims, then you not only *should* refuse, you are *bound* to refuse by the moral law.

We cannot say, as many Nazis did at the end of World War II, "I was only following orders." That does not get one off the hook for doing an immoral act.

Chapter 11
Catholic Prayer and Worship

Question #182

"How do you know when God is talking to you?" Mary C., 14

A. The more we pray and be silent, the more we can know what God's will is for our lives. God also reveals His will to us through signs, both small and large. So, keep an eye open for unique occurrences, answered prayers and an overall peace which comes about when we've made good choices.

Most importantly, God speaks to us through His Word. This Word comes to us in Jesus Christ (John 1:1), who is the Word made flesh, through the Bible and through Sacred Tradition as passed on by the Church (2 Thess. 2:15).

Question #183

"How can you increase your desire to know God?" Caitlin H., 15

A. Through prayer and study. It is through prayer

that God will give you the grace to know, love and serve Him. By study, you can learn more about Him. When you begin the learning process, you'll quickly find that the study of God is fascinating. The more you learn, the more you'll want to learn.

Because God is the Author of all things, He knows everything about everything. Therefore, the study of God and His interaction with the world *has* to be interesting. In fact, I believe the study of the things of God will be the most rewarding endeavor you will undertake.

Question #184

"If one person prays morning, noon and night and another person only once a week, does God value His relationship with the one more than the other? If so, which one? Jody G., 16

A. God is closer to those who are closer to Him. While praying three times a day rather than once a week doesn't *necessarily* make a person closer to God — one can have the wrong motive for prayer — all other things being equal, the person who prays more is closer to God.

Question #185

"If our lives are already planned out by God, why do we try to change our lives through prayer?" Jody G., 16

A. Our lives aren't "planned out by God" if you mean we have no freedom. God isn't "in time" (He's eternal and timeless), so in that sense He doesn't know "in advance" what will happen, He simply knows what is happening, for every moment is equally "now" to the Eternal God — past, present and future.

Yet, it is easier for our limited minds to think of God as knowing the future. So we say that God knows what will happen to us tomorrow, but we don't. That doesn't mean that what happens isn't influenced by prayer. For God not only knows what will happen tomorrow but He also knows your prayer and can allow it to influence the outcome of things just as He allows your other actions to shape events.

Prayer *does* help determine events. Prayer is like a fork in the road. If you choose a certain path or decision, you will have a certain outcome. If you don't choose a path (i.e., don't pray), you may not have the same outcome. So, it is a very good thing to pray. Your prayer will, in many cases, change the outcome of your future. We also believe God helps those who turn to Him more in prayer.

Prayer teaches us to direct our lives towards God and to depend on Him. Prayer helps us trust in "providence," which is God's plan for the world and our interaction with that plan.

Question #186

"Must you make the sign of the cross before you begin any type of prayer?" Charity W., 17

A. No. God is looking at your heart more than your physical action in prayer. He hears your prayer just as well if you don't make the sign of the cross. However, some actions predispose *us* more towards prayer like certain postures in sports make for a better performance. This is the case with making the sign of the cross. The sign of the cross can prepare us better for prayer.

Because the cross was the means by which the Savior was killed, the early Christians used to make the sign of the cross as a means of recognizing each other in times of persecution. Many of the early Christians write of the value of making the sign of the cross. St. Ephrem the Syrian in the year 306 says: "Mark all you do with the sign of the life-giving cross. Do not go out from the door of your house until you have signed yourself with the sign of the cross. Do not neglect to make that sign when you are eating or drinking, or going to sleep, whether you are at home or on a journey."

Making the sign of the cross, then, is a holy practice which Catholic Tradition upholds. You should try to remember to use it in prayer.

Question #187

"Why are Catholics the only ones who say the 'Hail Mary' and who pray to saints?" Rebecca B., 15

A. Catholics aren't the only ones. The Eastern Orthodox churches and some Anglicans also pray the Hail Mary and invoke the saints.

Why don't most Protestants? At the time of the Protestant Reformation in the 16th century, some of their leaders objected to what seemed to them to be an unjustified emphasis on Mary and the saints to the detriment of proper devotion to Christ. To be fair, there may well have been Catholics who didn't understand their Faith well and consequently who did have wrong ideas about the Blessed Mother and the other saints. But that was an abuse, and we shouldn't "throw the baby out with the bath water." The proper response to wrong devotion to Mary and the saints is right devotion, not no devotion at all. The Blessed Mother and the saints are powerful members of Christ's Mystical Body, the Church. As such, they can help us grow closer to Jesus.

Question #188

"What is the use of praying the rosary every day?" Sarah P., 15

A. Faithful repetition of the rosary brings peace to our heart and abundant grace to our soul. Praying the rosary inspires our heart with a more sincere love for the Blessed Trinity and Our Lady. When we meditate on the 15 mysteries of the rosary, we grow in love and understanding of the joyful, sorrowful and glorious events in Jesus' life. And anytime we can reflect on Jesus, we are sure to grow in holiness.

You may hear some Protestants teach that repetitious prayer, like the rosary, is condemned by Jesus in St. Matthew's Gospel (Matt. 6:7). This is not true. What is condemned in that verse is "vain" repetition. This is careless repetition, not heart-felt repetition. This verse was condemning a specific ritual of invoking pagan gods with a litany of special names, not the rosary, which wasn't developed for another 1,000 years.

Regarding repetitious prayer, Jesus Himself prayed the same prayer three consecutive times to His Father in the Garden of Gethsemene (Matt. 26:39-44). Also, the angels in heaven are continually saying, "Holy, Holy, Holy is the Lord God almighty" (Rev. 4:8). Repetition is not condemned, only mindless or vain prayer is.

Question #189

"Why is it so important to go to Mass?" Jeff D., 14

A. The Eucharist is the supreme act of worshiping

God because it is Christ offering Himself to the Father on our behalf. It is the sacrifice at Calvary 2,000 years ago made present here and now. By participating at Mass, we make Christ's sacrifice our own and receive the grace of salvation anew. When we receive the Eucharist, we receive Jesus Himself.

We also have an obligation to worship the Creator. It would be an insult to receive all the gifts we have received from God (our eyesight, our health, nice home, etc.) and then give Him nothing in return.

Here's an analogy: Let's say God gave a man $168 dollars to live on each week. The man had to pay $56 in rent and $56 for food and living expenses. The remaining $56 would be his to spend in any way. Then lets say that God asked for just $1 of the remaining $56. Wouldn't it be really selfish if the poor man said "no" to giving God the $1 He requested?

Well, God gives us 168 hours of life each week. We have to go to school or work for approximately 56 hours each week, and we have to sleep another 56 hours. But then we have 56 hours to do whatever we want! Isn't it selfish if we will not give Him at least one hour of worship each week?

Question #190

"Why can't they make church service more fun?" Jennifer M., 14

A. Why can't they make teenagers more serious? Since when is "fun" the most important thing in life? If someone lives life simply to "have fun," that person will end up being very selfish and, most likely, quite unhappy. It is only when we get out of ourselves and live for others that we truly find peace.

Knowing, loving and serving God and our neighbor is why we are here on earth. When one builds a life on the more important things, going to Mass and worshiping God becomes easier — actually, it becomes something we long to do. Focusing solely on our needs is empty and unfulfillng.

Question #191

"Why is Mass boring?" Philip T., 15

A. The are at least four reasons why people, especially the young, are bored at Mass:

(1) Because most people don't understand what *really* happens at Mass. When we actively listen to the Word of God at Mass, we receive encouragement, wisdom and guidance. When we receive the Eucharist in a state of grace, we are preparing our soul for its final destination — eternal happiness and peace in heaven.

If we really understood the amazing things that were happening at Mass, we would have greater interest.

(2) Because many think they are at Mass to be entertained. We are not. We are there to worship God and give back to Him the honor and glory He is due.

(3) Because people haven't been taught the Faith in an effective manner. Poor catechesis often leads to apathy about the things of God and love for things of the world.

(4) Because we are addicted to excitement and entertainment from watching and listening to too much television and pop music. We are an over-stimulated society. The advertising professionals know this. This is why they have reduced TV commercials to as little as 15 seconds in length. When we begin to slow down, we will begin to appreciate the more sublime riches in life, such as the Mass.

Question #192

"How long before Mass should we abstain from eating?" Jolene N., 17

A. The Church requires we abstain from eating for one hour before receiving the Eucharist. This is to prepare us to receive Jesus with greater yearning. It's only appropriate that we should prepare ourselves for receiving the Creator of the universe. Besides, it just doesn't seem right to have a chocolate doughnut or a cheeseburger in our stomach just a few minutes before we receive Jesus.

Question #193

"What should you get out of Church (Mass)?" Sean T., 16

A. The real question is, "What should you put into Mass?" We are there to worship God. He is not there to entertain us. With good and fervent worship of God and heart-felt prayer, you will have an inner peace in knowing you are adoring God and giving Him thanks.

Chapter 12
Miscellaneous Questions

Question #194

"Are people ever reincarnated?" Elisabeth G., 16

A. No. The Bible teaches that it is appointed to man once to die and then face judgement (Heb. 9:27). Ultimately, we will go to either heaven to be with God forever, or to hell, which is eternal exile from God's loving presence. Of course, on the way to heaven we may have to be purified in purgatory. But, in any case, there is no reincarnation.

Reincarnation denies the need for the Savior. Titus 3:5 says that we are not saved by works of righteousness, but by the renewal offered by the Holy Spirit. Reincarnation is a philosophy that says we have to continually "work" to improve ourselves, thus allowing us to come back to life as something better than before. In reincarnation, the death of Christ for our sins has no meaning because our salvation is totally dependent on our work.

246 Did Adam & Eve Have Belly Buttons?

Reincarnation also denies the dignity of the person as a unique individual being. You are not really unique if you are the reincarnation of George Custer and, before that, Cleopatra. You're a just a recycled person, not the unique "one time" creation made in the image and likeness of God.

Question #195

"Does the Church believe in life on other planets?" Andy D., 13

A. It doesn't officially teach anything on the matter. There is no biblical evidence for or against life on other planets. However, if there is, our God is their God, for there is only one God.

If there were other intelligent life forms, the next question would be: "Did they fall through sin like Adam and Eve or are they still in a pristine, unfallen state?" If they did fall, then they too would be in need of the Messiah to reconcile themselves with God the Father.

If there is life on other planets, it poses no challenge to the Catholic Faith. The salvation story still applies to us. We still need to pursue holiness and heaven.

C.S. Lewis wrote a space trilogy which considers some of the implications of extraterrestrial life. This might make for good reading if you're seriously interested in the question. The books are: *Out of the Silent Planet*, *Perelandra* and *That Hideous Strength*.

Question #196

"How will I know God is calling me to the priesthood?" Nathaniel D., 15

A. The first thing I would recommend is that you talk to a few priests and ask them how they knew the priesthood was their calling. Be sure to pray for discernment before and after your conversations with these men. You should also ask yourself the following questions:

Do I have an interest in the priesthood? Am I interested in the priesthood for my own glory or is my desire for some greater good, such as the salvation of souls? Do I find that I have a particular gift that matches the charisms of a particular order? Do I have a certain detachment from secular life? (This does not necessarily mean you are against marriage or a career, but you could sacrifice these for a greater good.) Am I attracted to a particular saint and do I have a desire to emulate him or her? Do I love the Church and am I willing to sacrifice for it and for the laity? Do I think I would be happy as a priest?

These are not all the questions you can ask yourself, but these can give you indications of whether you have a vocation to the priesthood or religious life.

If you believe you might have a call to the priesthood, consider going on a vocation discernment weekend. You are not "signing up" for the priesthood, but rather putting yourself in an environment where you can better discern. This will give you time with seminarians and priests. You will see the positive aspects of the priesthood, which are not often portrayed in the mass media. You will also have the chance to ask questions about the challenges they face, including celibacy, and be able to pray in nurturing surroundings.

Be sure to consider a religious order or diocesan program that is supportive of Church teaching. The future Church is one that is orthodox in its theology and dynamic in its application. The despair found in some seminaries and religious orders that are outspoken against Church teaching may turn some men, who genuinely have vocations, away from their vocations because they see a distorted view of the priesthood. Choose carefully and pray for discernment.

Question #197

"Do you have to follow a vocation if you know you have one? Are there consequences if you don't?" Caitlin H., 15

A. Everyone has a "genuine vocation," so it is not a question of *if* you have one but *what* it is. At the very least, we're all called to the general vocation of holiness. What we typically think of as vocations — married life, priesthood, religious life, etc. — are specific ways we are to fulfill the universal vocation to holiness.

Not following the specific vocation God has given you doesn't mean you can't be saved or even that your life will automatically be an irredeemable disaster. But the surest way to lasting peace and fulfillment in this life and heaven in the next is to follow your vocation as best you can discern it.

Deliberately opposing or ignoring your vocation *can* cause problems. Why? Because God has called you to do something and has given you special graces to help you do it. Opposing or ignoring that can limit your ability to grow in grace and do His will.

For example, let's say a man is called to the married life, but has a mild fascination with the priesthood which he pursues. Once ordained, he may grow resentful or struggle greatly with celibacy because he was not meant to live in that state. Conversely, let's say a man mistakes physical attraction for love and, subsequently, marries. Later, when he has had time to reflect on marriage, he realizes he really doesn't love his wife and was called to the priesthood. He may despair and jeopardize his salvation.

Of course these extreme situations needn't be the case, even for someone who doesn't follow his true calling. God's grace can overcome even that. But why settle for "Plan B" when God, Who is all-wise, has set out "Plan A" for you?

Question #198

"Why is there such a void in the number of musicians who play contemporary Christian music vs. mainstream music?" Kevin M., 18

A. There are at least two reasons: (1) Because there's much money and fame to be had in the secular (non-religious) world. (2) Because not many young people seem committed to the sacrificial life required by Christianity. We will start seeing more young people get involved with Christian music when we see more young people commit their lives to Jesus Christ.

You'll be glad to know that both the Catholic and Protestant Christian music market is growing.

Question #199

"Why can't the Bible be translated into English so that young people today can understand?" Joey K., 15

A. It has been. There is one Bible called the *International Student Bible for Catholics* which you can get from the people at YOU! magazine. I've listed the magazine's address in the "Resources" section.

One problem with Bibles that try to be "hip" or contemporary is that the meaning of some of the texts gets lost in the translation. Translations are sometimes so concerned with being relevant to the young generation that they compromise the integrity of the text. This can be spiritually dangerous in some cases.

You would probably be better off to look for a good priest or youth minister who knows the Scriptures and his Catholic Faith to lead a Bible study.

Question #200

"As a youth, I feel alone and left out of the Church. Are we truly welcome to be a part of the parish family?" Michelle P., 15

A. Yes, according to Jesus you are not only welcome, but of great importance. It was He who said: "Let the children come to Me" (Matt. 19:14). Now whether this actually takes place in your parish is another matter. I certainly hope your parish is making an effort to reach out to you.

If your parish is like most parishes, the pastor and religious educators are greatly concerned about the spiritual, mental and physical well-being of youth. After all, you are the future of the Church.

If there are no specific programs for youth, I suggest you get together some like-minded friends and meet with the pastor. He will appreciate your enthusiasm and may welcome your assistance.

Prayer to Follow Jesus

*Lord Jesus Christ, You have revealed Yourself
in Holy Scripture as the Way,
the Truth, and the Life.*

*Show me the way, show me the truth,
and grant me eternal life.*

*I accept You this day as my personal Lord and
Savior. Yours is the only name under heaven by
which man is saved. With Your grace,
I promise to turn from sin and live for You
from this day forth.*

*I pledge to become an active soldier for You and
the Catholic Church You established. Should I
fall into sin, I ask to be quickly
reconciled to You through the
Sacrament of Confession.*

*Through the intercession of the Blessed Virgin
Mary, I ask You to come into my heart and to
never leave me.*

Amen.

_____   _____
Signature   Date

Acknowledgements

Thank you to my editor **Mark Brumley, M.T.S.** who spent countless hours going over this work (and who kept me from slipping into heresy). You are a good friend and skilled theologian.

Thank you also to **mom** and **dad**; to my brother **Albert Pinto** for laying the theological foundation; to **Fr. C. John McCloskey, S.T.D., Patrick Madrid, Dr. Edward Peters, J.C.D., J.D.** and **Brian Simboli, Ph.D.** for technical assistance; to **Mark Ablett, Elena Bucchiarelli, Charles Harvey**, and **Tracy Moran** for proofreading assistance; and to my friend and brother-in-Christ, **Danny Pope**, whose questions and charitable challenges awakened me to the salvation found in Jesus and His Church.

A Guide to Confession

On the evening of His resurrection from the dead, Jesus appeared to His Apostles and gave them the power to forgive all human sins. Breathing upon them, He said, "Receive the Holy Spirit. If you forgive anyone's sins, they are forgiven. If you retain anyone's sins, they are retained" (Jn. 20:22-23). Through the Sacrament of Holy Orders, bishops and priests of the Church receive the ability from Christ Himself to forgive sins. It is exercised in the Sacrament of Reconciliation, also known as the Sacrament of Penance or simply as "Confession." Through this Sacrament, Christ forgives the sins that the members of His Church commit after Baptism.

When you enter the place set aside for the celebration of the Sacrament of Reconciliation, the priest may greet you and together you will make the sign of the cross. He may then choose a brief reading from the Bible to help you feel the merciful presence of Christ.

Next, you will begin with something like "Bless me, Father, for I have sinned. It has been (length of time) since my last confession. I wish to confess the following." You then tell your sins simply and honestly to the priest. The simpler and more honest the better! Don't make excuses! Don't try to disguise or minimize what you have done! Most importantly, think of Christ crucified dying out of love for you. Step on your pride and admit your guilt!

Remember, God wills that you confess all mortal sins by name and number. For instance, "I committed adultery three times and helped a friend procure an abortion" or "I missed Mass on Sunday."

This Sacrament is not only for the forgiveness of mortal sins. You may also confess your venial sins. The Church encourages devotional confession, that is, the frequent confession of venial sins as a means of growing perfect in the love of God and neighbor.

After you confess your sins, listen to the advice the priest offers you. You may also seek his help and guidance. He will then give you a penance, and ask you to either pray, fast or perform an act of charity. Through the penance, you begin to make reparation for the harm your sins have caused you, others and the Church. The penance of the priest reminds us that we need to be one with Christ in his sufferings so as to share in his resurrection.

Finally, the priest will ask you to express your sorrow for the sins confessed in an act of contrition. You can respond with something like: "Oh my Jesus, I am truly sorry for my sins and, with Your grace, make a firm amendment to sin no more." Then, exercising the power of Christ, the priest will give you absolution. As he prays over you, know with the certainty of faith that God is forgiving all your sins, healing you and preparing you for the Banquet of the Kingdom of Heaven! The priest will dismiss you saying: "Give thanks to the Lord for He is good." You respond: "His mercy endures forever." Or he may say: "The Lord has freed you from your sins. Go in peace" to which you answer, "Thanks be to God." Try to spend some time in prayer, thanking God for his forgiveness. Perform the penance the priest has given you as soon as possible after receiving absolution.

If you make good use and frequent use of this Sacrament, you will have peace of heart, purity of conscience and a deep union with Christ in His love for His Father and for all men and women. The grace of the Sacrament will cause you to become like Jesus, our Lord, in all you say and do! It will make you a stronger and more committed member of His Church!

In order to receive the Sacrament of Reconciliation worthily, the penitent (the sinner) must be sorry for his or her sins. Sorrow for sins is called contrition. Imperfect contrition is sorrow for sins motivated by fear of the fires of hell or the ugliness of sin itself. Perfect contrition is sorrow for sin motivated by the love of God.

Contrition, perfect or imperfect, must include a firm purpose of amendment, that is, a solid resolution to avoid the sin committed as well as the persons, places and things that prompted you to commit the sin in the first place. Without this repentance, contrition is insincere and our confession is pointless.

Whenever you sin, you should beg God for the gift of perfect contrition. Often God gives this gift when a Christian thinks about Jesus' agony on the cross and realizes that his sins are the cause of that suffering. Throw yourself into the arms of the crucified Savior's mercy and resolve to confess your sins to a priest as soon as possible.

When you come to Church to confess your sins, you should first examine your conscience. Review your life to see how you offended the good God since your last confession. The Church teaches that all mortal sins committed after Baptism must be confessed to a priest in order to be forgiven. This "precept" or law is of Divine Institution. Simply stated, this means the Confession of grave sins to a priest is part of God's plan and therefore is supported and carried out in the life of the Church. The *Catechism of the Catholic Church* (#1455) underscores the therapeutic value of confession for all believers.

Mortal sin is a direct, conscious and free violation of one or another of the Ten Commandments in a serious matter. Mortal sin, also known as grave or deadly sin, destroys the life of grace in your soul. God's grace begins to draw the sinner back to Him through sorrow for sin. He is brought back to life when he confesses his sins to a priest and receives absolution (forgiveness). The Church recommends that Catholics confess their venial sins which are violations of God's law that do not sever the relationship with Him or destroy the life of grace in the soul.

> — *Fr. Frederick L. Miller, S.T.D., teaches theology at*
> *St. Charles Borromeo Seminary*
> *Wynnewood, Pennsylvania.*

Examination of Conscience

The following will help you prepare for confession. If you are not sure whether your sins are "mortal" or "venial," the confessor will help you understand the difference. Don't be shy: Seek his assistance and ask questions! You always have the right to confess your sins face-to-face or "anonymously" behind a screen. The Church wants to make it as easy as possible for you to make a frank, honest confession of your sins. Most parishes schedule confessions on Saturday. You can also make an appointment for confession.

1. I am the Lord your God. You shall not have strange gods before me.

-Do I seek to love God with my whole heart and soul? Does He truly hold the first place in my life?

-Have I been involved with the occult or superstitious practices?

-Have I ever received Holy Communion in the state of mortal sin?

-Have I told a lie in confession or deliberately withheld confessing a mortal sin?

2. You shall not take the name of the Lord your God in vain.

-Have I insulted God's holy name or used it lightly or carelessly?

-Have I wished evil on anyone?

3. Remember to keep holy the Lord's Day.

-Have I missed Mass deliberately on Sunday, the Lord's Day or on Holy Days of obligation?

-Do I try to keep Sunday as a day of rest?

4. Honor your father and your mother.

-Do I honor and obey my parents? Do I care for them in their old age?

-Have I neglected my family responsibilities to spouse and children?

-Is my family life centered around Christ and his teaching?

5. You shall not kill.

-Have I murdered or physically harmed anyone?

-Have I had an abortion? Have I encouraged an abortion?

-Have I abused drugs or alcohol?
-Have I mutilated myself through any form of sterilization?
-Have I encouraged others to have themselves sterilized?
-Have I harbored hatred, anger or resentment in my heart towards anyone?
-Have I given scandal to anyone by my sins, thereby leading them to sin?

6. You shall not commit adultery.
-Have I been unfaithful to my marriage vows in action or thought?
-Have I practiced any form of artificial contraception in my marriage?
-Have I been engaged in sexual activity with a member of the opposite sex or the same sex?
-Have I masturbated?
-Have I indulged in pornographic material?
-Am I pure in my thoughts, words, actions? Am I modest in dress?
-Am I engaged in any inappropriate relationships?

7. You shall not steal.
-Have I taken what is not mine?
-Am I honest with my employer/employee?
-Do I gamble excessively thereby robbing my family of their needs?
-Do I seek to share what I have with the poor and needy?

8. You shall not bear false witness against your neighbor.
-Have I lied, gossiped or spoken behind anyone's back?
-Have I ruined anyone's good name?
-Do I reveal information that should be confidential?
-Am I sincere in my dealings with others or am I "two-faced?"

9. You shall not desire your neighbor's wife.
-Am I envious of another's spouse or family?
-Have I consented to impure thoughts? Do I try to control my imagination?
-Am I reckless and irresponsible in the books I read and the movies I watch?

10. You shall not desire your neighbor's goods.
-Am I envious of the possessions of others?
-Am I resentful and bitter over my position in life?

— Fr. Frederick L. Miller, S.T.D.

Resources

Here are a list of apostolates, magazines, books or encyclicals mentioned within this book:

Apostolates/Institutions

Courage, 424 W. 34th St., New York, NY 10001. Founded by Fr. John Harvey, this ministry offers support to the Catholic with a homosexual orientation who is striving to live a chaste life.

Real Love, Inc., 1520 W. Warner Rd., #106-138, Gilbert, AZ 85233, (602) 812-1194. Apostolate founded by Mary Beth Bonacci dedicated to promoting chastity, pro-life and pro-family message through seminars, tracts, books and tapes.

St. Joseph Communications., P.O. Box 720, West Covina, CA 91793. Phone: 818-331-3549. Publishes cassette tapes by Dr. Scott Hahn, Kimberly Hahn, Bishop Fulton Sheen, Jeff Cavins, Jesse Romero, and many others.

Thomas Aquinas Psychological Clinic, 16542 Ventura Blvd., Ste. 416, Encino, CA 91436, 818-789-4440, www.narth.com. Assists the person with a homosexual orientation to re-discover his or her true heterosexual identity using reparative therapy.

Authors

Chesterton, G.K.— The works of G.K. Chesterton can be found at www.chesterton.org or by writing The American Chesterton Society, 4117 Pebblebrook Circle, Minneapolis, MN, 55437.

Lewis, C.S. — The works of C.S. Lewis can be found at www.cslewis.org or by calling the C.S. Lewis Foundation at 888-CSLEWIS.

Sheed, Frank — Books by Frank Sheed's are available through various publishers. Some of may be found at www. evangelization. com.

Books/Booklets

100 Answers to Your Questions on Annulments by Edward J. Peters, J.C.D., J.D., 1997. Basilica Press, P.O. Box 510870, New Berlin, WI 53151-0870. Phone: 888-396-2339.

The Bible and the Catholic Church, Rev. Peter Stravinskas, 1996. Ignatius Press, 2515 McAllister St., San Francisco, CA 94118. Phone: 415-387-2324.

The Catechism of the Catholic Church. Doubleday Publishers, 1994. Or it can be purchased over the internet at www.evangelization.com

Darwin on Trial, Phillip E. Johnson, 1993. InterVarsity Press, P.O. Box 1400, Downers Grove, IL 60515, (630) 887-2500Or it can be purchased over the internet at www.amazon.com.

Darwin's Black Box, Michael J., Behe, 1996. The Free Press, New York, NY. It can be purchased over the internet at www.amazon.com.

The Faith by Fr. John Hardon, S.J., 1995. Servant Books, Box 8617, Ann Arbor, MI 48107. Or it can be purchased over the internet at www.amazon.com.

Healing the Homosexual, Dr. Joseph Nicolosi. Write or call: 16542 Ventura Blvd., Ste. 416, Encino, CA 91436, 818-789-4440.

The Homosexual Person, Father John Harvey, 1987. Ignatius Press, 2515 McAllister St., San Francisco, CA 94118, 1-970-221-3920. Or it can be purchased over the internet at www.evangelization.com

How the Bible Come To Us, J.M. Casciaro and J.L. Navarro, Sceptor Publishers, Box 1270, Princeton, NJ 08542, 800-322-8773.

International Student Bible for Catholics. Available through YOU! Magazine, 31194 LaBaya Drive, Suite 200, Westlake Village, CA 91362, (818) 991-1813.

Real Love, Mary Beth Bonacci, 1996. Ignatius Press, 2515 McAllister St., San Francisco, CA 94118, 1-970-221-3920. Or it can be purchased over the internet at www.evangelization.com

A Short History of the Catholic Church, Jose Orlandis. Contact Catholic Answers, P.O. Box 17490, San Diego, CA 92117 or call 619-541-1131.

Theology for Beginners. Frank J. Sheed, 1958, 1976. Servant Books, Box 8617, Ann Arbor, MI 48107. Or it can be purchased over the internet at www.evangelization.com

The Truth About Homosexuality, Father John Harvey, 1996. Ignatius Press, 2515 McAllister St., San Francisco, CA 94118, 1-970-221-3920. Or it can be purchased over the internet at www.evangelization.com

Where We Got the Bible, Rev. Henry Graham. Published by Catholic Answers, P.O. Box 17490, San Diego, CA 92177. Phone: 619-541-1131.

Why Wait, Josh McDowell and Dick Day. Here's Life Publishers, 1994. P.O. Box 1576, San Bernardino, CA 92402.Or it can be purchased over the internet at www.amazon.com

Magazines

Envoy Magazine, 3050 Gap Knob Rd., New Hope, KY 40052, 1-800-55-ENVOY.

YOU! Magazine, 31194 LaBaya Drive, Suite 200, Westlake Village, CA 91362, (818) 991-1813.

Encyclicals/Papal letters

Humanae Vitae (Of Human Life), *On the Pastoral Care of Homosexual Persons, Ordinatio Sacerdotalis* (Apostolic Letter Reserving the Priesthood to Men Alone), and *Women: Teachers of Peace.*

These encyclicals or letters can be retrieved by visiting www.ewtn.com or www.listserv.american.edu/catholic/church/papal/papal.html. Or you can purchase them through the Daughters of St. Paul, 50 St. Paul's Ave., Boston, MA 02130, (617) 522-8911.

Bibliography

Books

- *The Catholic Answer*, Book #2, Rev. Peter Stravinskas, Ph.D., S.T.L., Our Sunday Visitor Books
- *Catholic Replies*, James J. Drummey, C.R. Publications
- *Catholic Sexual Ethics*, Rev. Ronald Lawler, O.F.M., Cap., Joseph Boyle, Jr., & William E. May, Our Sunday Visitor Books
- *The Catechism of the Catholic Church*
- *Chastity, A Guide for Teens and Young Adults*, Rev. Gerald Kelly, S.J.
- *Everything You Ever Wanted To Know About Heaven*, Peter Kreeft, Ignatius Press
- *The Faith*, Rev. John Hardon, S.J., Charis/Servant Books
- *Hell*, Rev. F.X Schouppe, S.J., TAN Books
- *Knowing the Truth about Heaven & Hell*, Harry Blamires, Servant Books
- *Purgatory*, Rev. F.X. Schouppe, S.J., TAN Books
- *Purgatory and Heaven*, J.P. Arendzen, D.D., Canterbury Books
- *The Question Box*, Rev. Bertrand L. Conway, C.S.P., Paulist Press
- *Radio Replies*, Vol. 1, 2, & 3, Rev. Leslie Rumble, M.S.C., Ph.D. & Rev. Charles Carty, TAN Books and Publishing, Inc.
- *Reincarnation: Illusion or Reality*, Rev. Edmond Robillard, O.P., Alba House
- *The Saint Joseph Baltimore Catechism*, Rev. Bennett Kelley, C.P., Catholic Book Publishing Co.
- *Theology for Beginners*, F.J. Sheed, Servant Books
- *Why Wait?: What You Need to Know About the Teen Sexuality Crisis*, Josh McDowell & Dick Day, Here's Life Publishers

Articles/Booklets/Lectures

- *Believe Well, Live Well*, Marianne K. Hering, Focus on the Family
- *A Christian Looks at Mormonism*, Rev. William J. Mitchell
- *The Devil: Does He Exist and What Does He Do?*, Rev. Delaporte, Society of Mercy
- *Do We Believe in the Devil?*, Rev. P.J. McHugh*
- *Eternal Life in Paradise*, La Civilta Cattolica
- *Evolution: A Catholic Perspective*, James B. Stenson, Scepter Books

- *The Great Promise of Our Lady of Fatima*, Daughters of St. Paul
- *How the Bible Has Come To Us*, J.M. Casciaro and J.L. Navarro, Scepter Booklets
- *Is There Really a Devil?*, Rev. William P. Saunders
- *John Corapi's Amazing Story*, Rev. John Corapi, The Mary Foundation
- *On the Pastoral Care of Homosexual Persons*, Congregation for the Doctrine of the Faith
- *The Papacy: Expression of God's Love*, Knights of Columbus, Catholic Information Service
- *Scriptural Texts for Catholic Doctrine*, John Francis Coffey
- *Teen Sexuality*, Barbara McGuigan, St. Joseph's Communications
- *Was St. Paul Sexist?*, Marie-Eloise Rosenblatt, R.S.M., and Ronald D. Witherup, S.S., Catholic Update
- *Watchmaker Newsletter*, Catholic Origins Society, Rev. David Becker
- *What Does the Maleness of Jesus Have to Do With Priesthood?*, Bishop Elden F. Curtiss, Helena, MT
- *What Heaven and Hell Mean to Me*, Rev. Francis Ripley
- *What the Devil!*, Nicholas Halligan, O.P.*
- *When God Calls*, Federico Suarez, Scepter Books
- *Why Do Catholics...?*, Rev. Paul Stenhouse, M.S.C., Ph.D.
- *Why Women Can't Be Priests*, Mary DeTurris*
- *Women: Teachers of Peace*, Pope John Paul II

*The articles noted were found on the Eternal Word Television Network (EWTN) web site

Index of Questions

Topic/Question

Topic/Question

Topic/Question

Topic/Question